# AIRCRAFT
## The Story of Powered Flight

**Bristol Fighter**
Known affectionately to many as the 'Brisfit',
machines of this type carried out the first operations
of the newly-formed Royal Air Force at dawn on
April 1, 1918.

Triune Press

1

# AIRCRAFT
## The Story of Powered Flight

### Illustrations by John Young

### Text by Peter Shephard

## Triune Press, London

**Martin PBM Mariner**
US Navy patrol bomber, first flown in 1939.

ISBN 0 85674 006 3
Published by
Triune Press, London, England
© Trewin Copplestone Publishing Ltd 1972
Colour origination by City Engraving Co (Hull) Ltd,
England
Printed in Great Britain by Sir Joseph Causton
& Sons Ltd, London and Eastleigh.

**BAC VC10 long-range military transport**

5

John Young

Compared with other forms of transport, the story of powered aircraft is the most rapid technical adventure ever known. Within the span of one lifetime, man has progressed from faltering hops just above the ground, and scarcely half the length of a Jumbo Jet, to regular visits to the moon.

This book illustrates the many and varied forms of craft which have been fashioned to surmount nature's obstacle and carry out the tasks which flying machines are uniquely able to perform. Their development is an epic story of ingenuity, patient experiment, trial and error, and eventual application in practice, to bring a better life to the people of the world.

The air is the highway of the twentieth century.

de Havilland Dragon Rapide

# Prelude to Kitty Hawk

From the dawn of history man dreamed of flying. He watched birds soaring in the sky and longed to do the same, but many thousands of years were to pass before dream could become reality, and in his frustration at being forever tied to the earth, he endowed gods and supermen with the power of flight that he longed for himself. The dream was world-wide and evidence for it ranges from the winged gods of Egypt and Greece to the incredible flying ships described in the ancient writings of the Indus valley and portrayed on the walls of Aztec temples.

One story of ancient aviators tells of Dædalus and his son Icarus, who made bird-like wings of wax and feathers to escape from the King of Crete. Unfortunately, the wings worked so well that Icarus was tempted to fly too close to the sun, which melted the wax and sent him falling to his death in the Mediterranean.

How many would-be aviators have been killed or maimed in attempting to emulate the feat of Dædalus and Icarus will never be known, but in historic records one can read again and again of men who put their trust in flimsy mechanical wings and leapt to their deaths from cliff top and castle turret.

Early in the sixteenth century, Leonardo da Vinci focussed his genius on the problem of flight. He designed a helical wing machine which was intended to screw its way vertically into the air, but he was thwarted by lack of a suitable power plant. He turned instead to the ornithopter, a machine which could emulate the wing movements of a bird and be capable of operation by the arm, leg and head movements of the pilot. The problem he set himself was insoluble: even with the benefit of modern technology it seems certain that the man-powered ornithopter will never fly.

During the lifetime of Leonardo, European children were playing with a toy known as the Chinese flying top. In one fifteenth-century painting of Madonna and Child, the Infant is shown about to pull a string to send the four-bladed top spinning into the air. It is ironical that in this toy, so like a modern helicopter rotor, and in another much older plaything, the Chinese kite, man already held the secrets of heavier-than-air flight. There is in fact evidence that the Chinese were constructing man-carrying kites many hundreds of years before the birth of Leonardo da Vinci, but it was not until the end of the eighteenth century that the significance of the kite was rediscovered.

It was the Englishman Sir George Cayley who devised a theory of flight based on the way a kite develops lift when held in a moving airstream. In 1804 he built a successful model glider which was, in essence, an ordinary kite mounted at a 6° angle of incidence on a five-foot pole. At the rear of the pole was an adjustable cruciform tail. Cayley wrote of this model 'it was very pretty to see it sail down a steep hill'.

In 1850 Cayley, then in his seventy-seventh year, constructed a full-size glider which achieved a place in history as the first heavier-than-air machine to support a human being in free-flight. It cannot strictly be referred to as 'man-carrying', as the pilot was a boy of ten! Three years later, it was the turn of Cayley's coachman to glide across a small valley near Brompton Hall, the home of the Cayley family. We are told that the coachman promptly resigned, complaining that he had been hired to drive and not to fly.

In 1846 William Samuel Henson, who described Sir George Cayley as 'the father of aerial navigation' designed the Aerial Steam Carriage. This remarkably modern-looking monoplane incorporated a double-surfaced cambered wing section, a fuselage-mounted engine driving twin pusher propellers and a tricycle undercarriage. A model of the Aerial Steam Carriage, with a span of twenty feet, was built in 1847 but it lacked power and was unable to sustain itself in flight. Henson, whose plans for an international airline had received wide publicity, now faced public ridicule. He became discouraged and emigrated to America. His co-worker John Stringfellow persevered and built a new model on the

**Lilienthal glider**
The German gliding pioneer Otto Lilienthal made many successful flights before a fatal accident in 1896.

Henson principle with a span of ten feet. Reports differ, but it seems likely that this model was also underpowered and incapable of sustained flight.

In 1857 a French naval officer, Félix Du Temple, tested a model of his monoplane design, powered first by clockwork and later by steam. This was the first model to take-off, fly at a constant height and land at a point not lower than the level of take-off. Seventeen years later, a full-size man-carrying version became the first h-t-a craft to leave the ground under its own power, but it was a very brief hop, almost certainly achieved after rolling down a slope to gather momentum.

A famous name came on the scene in 1867 when Otto Lilienthal experimented with an unsuccessful ornithopter. Many years later, when he turned his attention to fixed wing gliders, he was to have a significant influence on the history of flight. Meantime, a Russian named Alexander Mozhaisky emulated Du Temple's brief hop after rolling down an inclined ramp in a one-ton machine powered by 30 hp steam engines. Other experimenters who succeeded in brief powered hops included Englishman Sir Thomas Moy, Clément Ader in France, and the famous American Sir Hiram Maxim who carried out his aviation experiments in England.

In 1890, Lilienthal began a series of gliding flights which finally established the practicability of h-t-a flight and which, by inspiration, led directly to the momentous flight at Kitty Hawk thirteen years later. Lilienthal completed more than two thousand successful flights and at the time of his death in 1896 he was preparing to attempt powered flight. The fatal crash was caused by loss of control in gusty conditions—control of Lilienthal gliders was achieved by moving the pilot's body to shift the centre of gravity. He was considering wing warping, air brakes and moveable rudders as means of improving control, but none of these devices had been tested in the air.

A young Englishman, Percy Pilcher, travelled to Berlin to meet Lilienthal and fly his gliders. Pilcher carried on with Lilienthal's work, and he too aimed at fitting a glider with a motor—a 4 hp petrol engine driving a five-foot diameter propeller. Sadly, before he could test this machine, he, too, was killed in a gliding accident following structural failure.

In America, meanwhile, Samuel Pierpoint Langley was building successful steam powered models. In 1896 his 14-foot tandem-wing 'Aerodromes' achieved sustained flights of 4200 feet and in 1901 he flew the first petrol-powered model to make a sustained flight. On December 7 and 8, 1903, a full-size 'Aerodrome' piloted by Charles M. Manely was launched twice over the Potomac River, but each time the machine fouled the launching catapult and fell into the water.

Now the race was almost run—nine days later Orville Wright would take-off on his flight into history.

# The Wright brothers

Wilbur and Orville Wright ran a modest bicycle business in Dayton, Ohio. Both had been interested in flying since boyhood and, through the early 1890s, they avidly followed the progress of Lilienthal. His death in 1896 crystalized their desire to follow in his footsteps, but it was not until 1899 that they built their first model. This was a 5-foot biplane kite designed to test wing warping as a method of control. In September 1900, their No. 1 glider was tested as a kite over the sand dunes of Kitty Hawk. A 17-foot span biplane with fixed forward elevator, it was flown mostly as an unmanned kite, but both men made manned kite flights and also performed their first free glides.

Well satisfied, they now built glider No. 2 with a similar configuration but with a span of 22 feet. Tests began on July 27, 1901, and continued into August, flights of up to 389 feet made in winds of over 25 mph.

Glider No. 3, first flown on September 20, 1902, had a span of 32 feet and was generally similar to Nos. 1 and 2, with the addition of twin fixed vertical fins, which were later changed to a single controllable rudder. In this machine, the brothers made almost a thousand flights in winds up to 35 mph. They were now by far the most experienced airmen in the world with an efficient aeroplane lacking only a powerplant.

As no suitable motor existed, the Wrights set about designing and building a 12 horse power petrol engine to power No. 4—the Wright Flyer. This machine followed the well-proven design of No. 3, but with a biplane forward elevator and twin vertical rudders. The span was 40 feet 4 inches and the motor drove twin contra-rotating propellers through bicycle chains.

First flight on December 14, 1903, was a failure. Due to over-control by Wilbur, the Flyer reared up, stalled and crashed. Fortunately, damage was slight and on December 17, Orville took the controls and ran the engine up to full power. At 1035 hours, in front of five local witnesses, Flyer moved down the launching track. After a run of some 40 feet it rose into the air and flew an undulating course for twelve seconds, touching down 120 feet from the point of lift-off.

Longer and smoother flights were carried out that day, but they were almost routine. That first take-off at 1035 had thrust an uncomprehending world into the aerospace age, and Orville's fluttering one-hundred-and-twenty-foot ride over the sands of Kitty Hawk was to prove, in the words of another famous airman, '. . . a giant leap for mankind'.

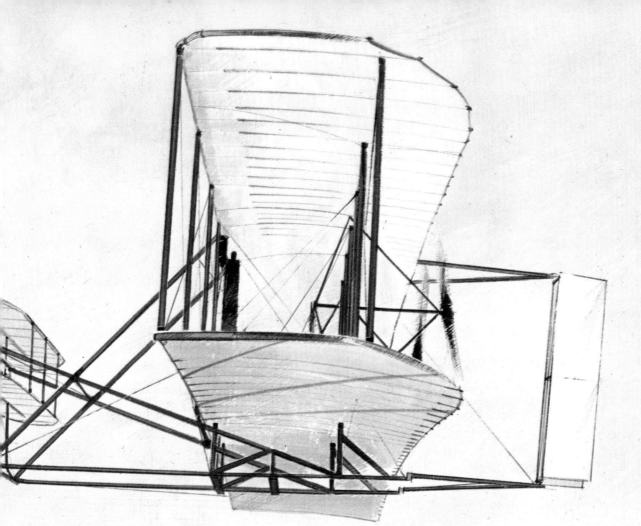

## The Wright brothers' Flyer
The first power-driven, controlled and sustained flight by man took place at Kitty Hawk, North Carolina, USA, on December 17, 1903. That afternoon, Orville Wright, who piloted the machine, telegraphed his father in Dayton, Ohio: "Success four flights Thursday morning all against twenty-one mile wind started from level with engine power alone average speed through air thirty-one miles longest fifty-nine seconds inform press home Christmas".

# 1903-1914

Incredible as it now seems, the world took little notice of the news from Kitty Hawk. In May 1904 the Wrights invited the press to a demonstration of their Flyer No.2. Unfortunately, they neglected to test the machine first, and in front of a crowd of sceptical reporters, No. 2 ran off the end of its launching track and shuddered to an ignominious halt. Thereafter editors were even less inclined to print eye-witness accounts of the Wright's activities. Disbelief extended to the armed forces—in October 1905, nineteen days after Flyer No. 3 had covered 24 miles non-stop, the US Board of Ordnance informed the brothers that the Army had no interest in aircraft until a machine was produced that could support a man in horizontal flight! Somewhat disillusioned, the Wrights put away their aeroplane for three years, and simply waited for the world to acknowledge them. They were confident that their lead could not be overtaken—but they were wrong. On the other side of the Atlantic aviation development was surging ahead, and on November 12, 1906 the airship pioneer Alberto Santos-Dumont covered 722 feet in 21 seconds in a heavier-than-air machine. A year later Louis Blériot flew a remarkable aeroplane—a shoulder-wing mono-plane with a partially enclosed fuselage, a tractor propeller and rear mounted elevator, the configuration that would be accepted as the norm thirty years later. This machine crashed in December, 1907, but Blériot was not discouraged—in the years ahead he was to establish something of a reputation for surviving crashes.

Another crash, on September 17, 1908, established an unhappy precedent when Lt. Selfridge of the US Army became the first passenger to die in an air crash. The machine was a Wright biplane piloted by Orville, who was seriously injured.

A major milestone in aviation history was reached on July 25, 1909, when Louis Blériot won a £1000 Daily Mail prize for the first powered crossing of the English Channel. He took off from a point near Calais at 04.40 hours and crash-landed in a field near Dover some forty minutes later. Blériot was welcomed enthusiastically, but many Englishmen had forbodings. The Channel—England's prime defence for 2,000 years—had been bridged at last.

In August 1910, the Hon. C. S. Rolls (of Rolls Royce) achieved the unhappy distinction of being the first British pilot to die in an air crash. The following year saw the first official air mail flight from Allahabad to Naini Junction in India, and almost every month now saw a significant extension of the aeroplane's capabilities. On March 23, Louis Bréguet carried eleven passengers over a distance of 15 kilometres and the following day a Sommer biplane lifted twelve passengers—albeit for only 800 metres. In April 1910, one Blériot machine flew non-stop from London to Paris and another flew non-stop Paris to Berlin.

More and more people were qualifying for pilot's licences. At the end of 1912, 2480 international certificates had been issued. Of these, 966 went to France, 382 to Britain, 335 to Germany and 193 to the United States.

1912 had seen the beginning of full-scale military aviation in Britain with the formation of the Royal Flying Corps, and naval aviation began with the take-off of a Short biplane from a make-shift flight deck on board HMS Africa. Also in 1912, Glen Curtiss, already established as a moving force in US aviation, flew the world's first flying boat, the first of a long line of world famous aircraft.

The 15th of April 1913 saw the first contest for a trophy presented by M. Jacques Schneider. It was won by a Deperdussin at a modest 45·75 mph but in the period between the two World Wars, the Schneider Trophy would play the most significant part in increasing the performance of both aeroplanes and their power plants. Maximum speeds of contest winners were to increase by a factor of almost ten and the ultimate winner, the Supermarine S6B, was to be the inspiration of the Spitfire. The Rolls Royce R engine, which powered the S6B, was the direct ancestor of the Merlin—one of the most widely-used aero engines of World War Two.

# War and Progress

When war began in 1914, the aeroplane was still in its infancy, and rag-bag squadrons of Wrights, Farmans and Blériots were impressed into service as the eyes of the ground forces. When fighting ended in November 1918, the aeroplane had come of age with purpose-designed warplanes performing a variety of tasks—interception, maritime reconnaissance, ground attack and long-range bombing. Some of these machines were to soldier on in military service for many years—the RAF, for example, would still be flying the Bristol Fighter in the early 1930s, while the Fokker D VII, perhaps the finest fighter produced in the war years, went into service with the United States Marine Corps.

Bomber development in the war years was to have far-reaching effects. In 1914, raids were carried out with 20lb bombs, but four years later the standard RAF heavy bomb weighed 1650 lb. The bombers designed to carry these weapons—the Handley Page 0/400 and the Vickers Vimy, provided a foundation for the development of international airlines and the Vimy in particular was to earn a place in history as the first aeroplane to fly non-stop across the Atlantic.

Aero-engine design during the war kept pace with the advances in aerodynamics and power outputs increased from around 80 hp to more than 400 hp. When peace returned, aero-engine industries were firmly established on both sides of the Atlantic and the names of Rolls Royce, Benz and Hispano had become synonymous with power in the air.

The armistice of November 11, 1918 silenced the war birds, but it was only a temporary lull and little more than two decades later the snarl of Rolls, Benz and Hispano engines would dispute again the same fated sky.

## Blériot
In 1909, the great French pioneer, Louis Blériot, became the first to cross the English Channel by powered aircraft.

# World War One

## Fokker D.VII
Winner of a competition to find a new fighter to attempt to gain air supremacy over the Western Front, the D.VII was one of the most potent aircraft of the war.

## Sopwith Camel
The Camel became a deadly weapon in the hands of a skilled pilot and was famous as the machine which destroyed more enemy aircraft than any other single type during the Great War.

**S.E.5A**
As easy to handle as the Camel was difficult, the S.E.5A became famous as the mount of aces of the calibre of Bishop, Mannock and McCudden.

# Early Civil Aviation

After the armistice, demobilised bombers were pressed into service for a wide variety of civil duties. In May 1919, a Handley Page 0/400 became the first aeroplane to receive a British certificate of airworthyness, and on August 25, 1919, a DH-4 flew the world's first scheduled airline service from London to Paris. The de Havilland DH-4 was to feature prominently in the story of early civil aviation. It was a favourite mount for the 'barnstormers' or exhibition flyers who did so much to kindle air-mindedness in the United States, and in more serious mood it was instrumental in establishing the US Air Mail. In September 1922, Lt. James H. Doolittle flew a modified DH-4 on the first one-day, coast-to-coast crossing of the U.S.A. His total time for the journey was 22 hours and 35 minutes, including a one-and-a-quarter-hour refuelling stop at Kelly Field in Texas. Yet another DH-4 made history when it was successfully refuelled in flight on June 27, 1923. The pilots were Captain L. H. Smith and Lt. J. P. Richter, and in June 1923, they established a world endurance record of 37 hours and 15 minutes. In the course of the record flight the DH-4 was refuelled in flight fifteen times.

But for a truly momentous moment in the history of civil aviation we must go back to December 12, 1915. On that day the Junkers J.1 took to the air for the first time. Nicknamed *Blechesel* or 'tin donkey', the J.1 was the world's first all-metal aeroplane—a stressed-skin monoplane with a top speed of 105 mph. The J.1 never carried a passenger and only a single example was built, but experience gained with it led directly to the Junkers J.13 low-wing monoplane, a six-seat, all-metal commercial transport with an enclosed cabin. The J.13, which made its first flight on June 25, 1919, has been described as one of the most significant aircraft ever built. It demonstrated the advantages and practicability of all-metal construction and remained in production for thirteen years—a total of three hundred and twenty-two being built for service around the world. Professor Junkers designed his all-metal transports to last—at least one J.13 survived to see service in World War 2, and the corrugated metal skin that characterised the machine became a Junkers trade mark, featuring later on the most famous of that company's transports, the Ju52 3M. Although an old lady herself when war came in 1939, the Ju52 served the Luftwaffe with distinction in every campaign. After the war it flew on British European Airways routes for several years and remained in service with the Swiss and Spanish air forces until the end of the 1960s.

## de Havilland D.H.4

Incredible feats of airmanship were performed in the barnstorming days of the aerial mail across the USA. Flying in all weathers, these brave pioneers marked out the airways of the future.

## Junkers F.13

One of the most significant commercial machines in the history of flying, the German F.13 was one of the first to be designed specifically as a transport and notable for its low-wing, all-metal construction and its enclosed cabin.

## Douglas World Cruiser

Four of these machines left Seattle on April 4, 1924 to attempt to circumnavigate the world. After epic adventures and the loss of two aircraft, the survivors returned to the starting point in September, having covered 26,345 miles.

## Fokker F.VIIb 3m

The first flight from America to Australia. Piloted by Charles Kingsford Smith, the 'Southern Cross' took off from Oakland, California, on May 31, 1928, and flew 7450 miles across the Pacific Ocean *via* Honolulu and Fiji to Brisbane, Australia. The 3114 miles from Hawaii to Fiji were the longest over-water flight that had ever been made.

## Vickers Vimy
The first non-stop transatlantic flight was made by this ex-bomber in June, 1919, by the two Britons, Alcock and Brown, who flew from Newfoundland to Ireland in sixteen hours. Similar machines made the first flights from England to Australia and South Africa.

## de Havilland D.H.60 Moth
The first solo flight from Britain to Australia was made in the Moth 'Jason' when Amy Johnson took off from Croydon (May 5, 1930) and landed nineteen days later at Darwin, Australia.

SOUTHERN CROSS

1985

**Ryan 'Spirit of St Louis'**
Charles Lindbergh in his Ryan monoplane
'Spirit of St Louis' flew the Atlantic alone, from
New York to Paris, in 33½ hours in May, 1927.

# The Pioneers

By 1918, the aeroplane was established as a major weapon of war—now it was the turn of a select band of aviators to prove its potential for peace. In May 1919, three Curtiss flying boats left Newfoundland to cross the Atlantic *via* the Azores. Only one completed the journey, but it proved that the aeroplane could link continents across 3000 miles of ocean.

In the following month, Alcock and Brown took off from Newfoundland in a Vimy to make the first non-stop crossing of the Atlantic and crash-land in an Irish bog sixteen hours later. The same year, another Vimy flew to London from Port Darwin, Australia in an elapsed time of twenty-eight days, while the British R-34 airship crossed the Atlantic non stop, east-to-west, in 108 hours.

On April 4, 1924, four Douglas World Cruisers named Seattle, Chicago, Boston and New Orleans took off from Lake Washington to circumnavigate the earth. Seattle crashed in mountainous country in Alaska and Boston came down in the Atlantic, but two machines completed the 27,534-mile flight in 175 days and returned to Seattle on September 28th.

Of all the early pioneers, Charles Lindbergh's exploit most vividly caught the public imagination. Back in 1919, Raymond Orteig had offered $25,000 for the first non-stop New York to Paris flight. First to make the attempt, in September 1926, was wartime ace René Fonck, but his heavily laden Sikorsky crashed on take-off killing two of the four man crew. In April 1927, two naval officers were also killed while testing their machine.

At 07.54 on May 20, 1927, Lindbergh waved 'chocks away' and began the long, nerve-wracking take-off from Roosevelt Field. His single-engined Ryan Monoplane was little bigger than a modern flying club aircraft and he flew solo without radio, parachute, sextant or dinghy. The fuselage was a flying fuel tank with 2750 lb of petrol for the Wright Whirlwind engine and five chicken-and-ham sandwiches for the pilot.

The overladen Ryan struggled reluctantly into the air and vanished in the morning mist. For more than a day the world heard nothing—and then an Irish fisherman saw the little monoplane scudding low over the water. The fatigue that had plagued Lindbergh throughout the crossing now left him and he flew steadily across Ireland and England. In the last light of day he saw the English Channel glinting below his nose—then the dark line of the French coast, the beacons of the London-Paris Airway—and at long, long last, the lights of Paris. To a tumultuous welcome, he touched down at Le Bourget 33 hours and 31 minutes after take-off, and as the Ryan rolled to a standstill there were still 85 gallons in the tanks.

In the following year, another epic over-water flight was made by Charles Kingsford Smith, piloting a Fokker Tri-motor named Southern Cross from Oakland, California to Brisbane, Australia, *via* Hawaii and Fiji.

Although the first three decades of powered flight had produced a number of women pilots, it was not until 1930 that a woman flyer hit the headlines around the world. In May of that year, a young girl not long out of flying school took off solo from Croydon, England in a second-hand DH 60 Moth. Nineteen days later, when she landed in Darwin, Australia, Amy Johnson and her Moth 'Jason' had become a part of aviation history.

# Balloons and Airships

The story of lighter-than-air craft began on October 15, 1783 when François Pilâtre de Rosier made man's first flight in a tethered hot-air balloon invented by the brothers Joseph and Etienne Montgolfier. In the same year, the first hydrogen balloon rose from the Champs de Mars in Paris and within two years a Frenchman, Jean-Pierre Blanchard, and an American, Dr John Jeffries, had made the first aerial crossing of the English Channel.

The ballon was, in itself, almost a dead end. It exists today only as a form of sport, a scientific recording vehicle, or a passive defence against low-flying aircraft. But it was the metamorphosis of hydrogen ballon into airship which first gave man the means to navigate in the air and land safely at a pre-determined destination.

In 1837, Sir George Cayley had outlined a plan for a streamlined balloon, or dirigible, with steam-driven propellers for propulsion and steering, and in 1852 Frenchman Henri Giffard flew a steam powered non-rigid airship from Paris to Trappes at a modest 5 mph.

Airship design was refined by such pioneers as Réaud and Krebs in France, by Dr Karl Wolfert in Germany, and by Brazilian Alberto Santos-Dumont who flew a petrol-engined dirigible around the Eiffel Tower in 1898. In the same year in Germany, the first rigid airship was taking shape under the eye of Count Ferdinand von Zeppelin. That ship was the first of a line which were to carry 35,000 passengers in safety on scheduled services *before* the outbreak of war in 1914.

Inevitably the achievements of Count Zeppelin were turned to the arts of war and his beautiful ships became the world's first strategic bombers, following the trail blazed across the English Channel by Blanchard and Jeffries a century and a half before.

When peace returned, the airship again took its place on the air lanes. Zeppelins from Germany and British ships such as the R34 and R100 made many successful long-distance voyages, including commercial crossing of the Atlantic. But a series of disasters, culminating with the blazing destruction of the Hindenburg, brought the airship story to an untimely close at a time when the availability of non-inflammable helium gas might have removed the one obstacle to safe profitable operation.

Today there is a growing interest in the possibility of giant airships for the transport of containerised cargo. With the prospect of efficient nuclear power and plentiful supplies of helium gas, we may once more witness the spectacle of vast silver ships sailing silently across the skies.

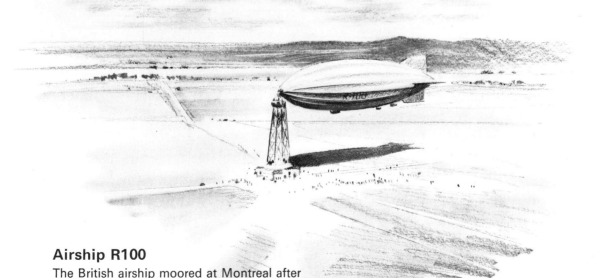

**Airship R100**
The British airship moored at Montreal after crossing the Atlantic in 1930.

## Grumman F3F

The F3F was in combat squadron service from 1936 until late 1941 and was regarded as the ultimate in biplanes by its pilots, who had a high regard for its delightful flying qualities.

## Bristol Bulldog

Between 1929 and 1937, Bulldogs wore the colourful liveries of ten RAF fighter squadrons.

## Curtiss BFC-2 Hawk

A Hawk from Bombing Squadron 2, USS Saratoga, 1933.

# The Heyday of the Biplane

## Hawker Hart
Chosen in 1930 as the standard light day-bomber of the RAF, the Hart proved to be one of the most adaptable biplanes ever to fly with the squadrons.

## Boeing P-12
More machines of the P-12 series were built between 1928 and the end of the biplane era than any other basic American military type, a record which stood until the eve of World War 2.

# From Biplane to Monoplane

The years that followed the armistice of 1918 have often been referred to as the heyday of the biplane, for although the potential of the monoplane was being demonstrated daily by such aircraft as the Junkers J.13, the air forces of the world remained true to the biplane, continually refining the breed until it reached a peak in the superbly manoeuvrable machines that were ideally suited to the aerial warfare of 1914-1918. At air displays, the crowds thrilled to the incredible aerobatics of such aircraft as the Bristol Bulldog and the Boeing P-12, but in reality the performance of such types showed little improvement over the Pups, Spads and Fokkers of the war years.

In 1931, the Royal Air Force re-equipped some squadrons with the Hawker Fury—a machine considered by many enthusiasts to be the ultimate in biplane design, and the first RAF fighter capable of speeds in excess of 200mph. But it was only marginally faster than the Hawker Hart day bomber then rolling off the production lines—and as the Fury squadrons worked up in Britain the Dornier 17 medium bomber was already taking shape in Germany. With a speed of 240 mph, the Do17 was considerably faster than any fighter in service anywhere and when it made its first flight in 1934 it was clear that the days of the biplane were numbered. The biplane protagonists were deeply entrenched, however, and machines such as the Gloster Gladiator and the Grumman F3F remained in front-line service even after the start of World War 2.

**Fairey Long Range Monoplane**
The world record for a straight-line distance was gained for Britain in February, 1933, when this machine flew 5341 miles from Cranwell, England, to Walfis Bay, SW Africa, in 57 hours 25 minutes non-stop.

**Bristol 138**
This all-wooden construction with a supercharged Bristol Pegasus engine, and with its pilot wearing a pressurised suit, reached a height of 53,937 feet in June, 1937 — establishing a world height record.

The early 1930s also saw the monoplane establishing itself as the pace-setter in civil aviation. In 1929, the Fairey long range monoplane had flown 4130 miles non-stop to India in 50 hours and 37 minutes, and in 1933, another Fairey LRM flew 5431 miles non-stop from England to South Africa. Other monoplanes were also making headlines. In Britain, the Bristol 138 carried man to the stratosphere and in America the Lockheed Vega airliner was setting new standards. In 1932, Amelia Earhart, flying a Vega, became the first woman to fly solo across the Atlantic, and in 1935 she made the solo crossing from Hawaii to California. Another Lockheed flown by Wiley Post made the first solo flight around the world *via* Berlin, Moscow, Irkutsk and Alaska.

On the world's airlines, too, the day of the biplane was nearly over. The Handley Page HP42 had established a reputation for comfort and reliability, but it was slow and passengers were already demanding shorter journey times.

British designers responded first with the Armstrong Whitworth Ensign and then with the de Havilland Albatross—four-motor monoplanes with retractable undercarriages. In America, the twenty-passenger Curtiss Condor biplane gave place to the Ford Tri-motor and ultimately to the Douglas Commercial monoplanes—the DC1, DC2 and DC3, which were to set the pattern of air travel for the next decade.

# The first real Airliners

## Ford Trimotor
In 1925, the Ford Motor Company entered the aviation arena with a three-engined transport designed by William Stout. This rugged machine, completely covered with corrugated metal, carried fourteen passengers.

## Douglas DC-3
'The airliner that changed the world'. Shown here is the first of more than 10,000 DC-3s, which made its initial flight in December, 1935. The DC-3 dominated the world of air transport and later served as a war transport, being described in a USAF citation as 'unquestionably the best single airplane ever built'.

**Handley Page H.P.42**
Built for Britain's Imperial Airways in the early
1930s, the majestic H.P.42 set new standards of
passenger comfort on the Air Mail route to Cape
Town and services from London to the capital
cities of Europe.

# Racing and Progress

### Gee Bee Racer
Designed in 1930, built in 1932, the Gee Bee found fame at the National Air Race Meet at Cleveland in 1932, when 'Jimmie' Doolittle won the Thomson Trophy at an average speed of 252·68 mph.

One of the stimuli to technical progress was provided by air racing. In the United States, the racing aeroplane became very highly specialised. Engines grew ever larger and more powerful while airframes shrank to the barest minimum that would support engine, fuel and pilot in flight. The ultimate was reached with the Gee Bee R1 of 1932, in which 'Jimmy' Doolittle won the Thompson Trophy at a speed of 252·7 mph.

Across the Atlantic, racing took a more practicable direction. The England to Australia race, for example, saw the development of the de Havilland Comet racer—a twin engined low wing monoplane which, in addition to taking first place, led directly to the very high performance Mosquito bomber of the World War 2. Similarly, the Schneider Trophy contests led to aviation developments which could not even have been guessed at when Monsieur Schneider instituted his trophy. The contests, spread over a period of eighteen years, saw the transition from biplane to monoplane and an eightfold increase in speed.

The first contest in 1913 was won by a Deperdussin at an average speed of 45·75 mph. By 1925, the winning speed had increased five times and the trophy was taken by Doolittle at an average of 232·5 mph. A British Gloster Napier came second at 199·169 mph, with a Macchi M33 third at 168·44 mph. Another British entry crashed during trials—this was the Supermarine S4, a revolutionary monoplane design that despite its misfortune showed the shape of contest winners to come.

The twelfth and final contest was held in 1931. If Britain could win three times running, she would gain the trophy outright, but the British government of the day decided not to enter. The situation was saved by a private benefactor, Lady Houston, who gave £100,000.

It was hoped that Britain, France, Italy and the USA would all enter, but in the event only Britain was represented. At 1300 hours on September 13, Flight Lieutenant Boothman carried out the preliminary sea trials in the S6B and then flew the course at an average of 340·08 mph, securing the Schneider Trophy permanently for Britain.

But the significance of this triumph did not end there. The Rolls Royce R engine that powered the S6B led directly to the Merlin, and R. J. Mitchell, designer of the Supermarine S seaplanes, applied the experience gained from the contests to the creation of a low-wing, single-engined fighter to counter the growing threat posed by German air power. In March 1936, that fighter took to the air and the Supermarine Spitfire was born.

### de Havilland Comet
Built especially for the 1934 England-Australia Air Race, the Comet 'Grosvenor House' won and brought the two countries to within three days flying time of each other.

# Famous Trainers

Flying training was a lonely business in the early days—like Lilienthal, Pilcher and the Wrights before them, the first pilots had to learn their own way in the air and every flight was a solo.

When aircraft were powerful enough to carry a passenger in addition to the pilot, students could be given air experience trips before making their first flight in charge. From this it was a small step to the dual control trainer and the system of flying training that has endured to the present day.

One of the first true trainer aircraft was the Avro 504, a robust tractor biplane which although it saw service both as a bomber and an observation machine, is best remembered as the aeroplane which taught the Royal Air Force to fly. More than 7000 were built and the Avro 504 remained in service long after the First World War had ended.

In the United States, the Curtiss Jenny was the first of a long line of trainer aircraft, including the Stearman PT 13 Kaydet and the Ryan PT 16 and PT 20—the machines on which thousands of allied pilots learned to fly in the Second World War. But perhaps the most famous trainer of them all was the North American NA-16, variously known as Harvard or Texan. Ordered in quantity for the British and Commonwealth training schools in 1938, the Harvard quickly gained a reputation as a first-class advanced trainer—and also as the noisiest aeroplane ever to fly with the Royal Air Force. It served as the standard British advanced trainer throughout the war and continued in large scale use until the 1950s. Under the name Texan it also served with the United States Air Force in large numbers and was delivered to the air forces of many other countries including Argentina, Peru, Belgium, Holland, Sweden and Nationalist China. Its rugged construction, designed to take the punishment of flying school service, fitted it well for other duties and in the years following the Second World War, the Harvard/Texan saw front-line service in a dozen minor wars from West Africa to South East Asia. As a ground attack bomber, armed with bombs, rockets and machine guns it achieved a reputation, like the Stuka before it, of terrorising the enemy with noise even before it unleashed its weapons.

## Supermarine S.6B
Outright winner of the Schneider Trophy contests and the first machine to push the world speed record beyond 400 mph.

## Avro 504
After an initial career during World War I as a fighter and bomber, the Avro 504 became one of the outstanding trainers of all time, remaining with the Royal Air Force until the early 1930s—a link between the days of sticks and string and those of the powerful metal monoplane.

## Boeing-Stearman PT-13 Kaydet
The Kaydet was the most widely used primary trainer of the US forces in World War 2.

## North American AT-6 Harvard
Known in US service as the Texan, the AT-6 is pre-eminent among advanced piston-engined trainers. Dating from the mid-1930s, this type is still in world-wide service with nearly forty air forces.

# The Age of the Flying Boat

More than any other type of aeroplane, the flying boat conjures nostalgic memories of golden days gone by—of a moment in time never to be recaptured. Anyone who has watched a big boat rise on the step and seen the white wake thin and die as she shook the water from her hull and rose majestically into the sky, will have known a magic with which a lumbering land plane can never compete.

Flying boats captured the public imagination in the First World War when they protected sea lanes from submarine and surface raider. Then in 1919, the Curtiss NC-4 spanned the Atlantic and inspired the long-range boats which laid the foundations of international air transport.

In the United States, Sikorsky and Boeing created the famous Clippers, while Germany produced the incredible Dornier DoX, a twelve-engined giant which on one flight lifted one hundred and sixty passengers and crew, plus a number of stowaways. The DoX made a greatly publicised Atlantic crossing by flying so low that the lift of its huge wing was augmented by the 'ground effect' between wing and sea. In recent years it has been suggested, unkindly, that the DoX may have some claim to be the world's first hovercraft.

From Britain, the C Class Empire flying boats linked the outposts of the British Empire and established a standard of comfort that is remembered to this day: the chosen few who flew with Canopus and her far-ranging sister ships will never be won over by the technological marvels of Jumbos and SSTs.

In the Second World War, the Sunderland and Catalina, descendants of Empire boats and Clippers, guarded the sea lanes as their predecessors had done in an earlier war—and it was a foolhardy U-Boat commander who failed to crash-dive when a patrolling flying boat appeared over the horizon. Even in air combat, the Sunderland earned the respect of its adversaries—with its power-operated turrets it was christened 'flying porcupine' by German aircrews.

## Short Empire Flying Boat

Imperial Airways launched the Empire Air Mail scheme which speeded mail services within the British Commonwealth. Mail and passengers were carried by the fleet of 28 Empire flying boats from 1937 until war broke out two years later. The Sunderland military derivative of this airliner played a notable part in the conflict.

When peace returned, it seemed that the flying boat had an assured future, and de-mobbed submarine hunters re-established the flying boat legend of the 1930s. Early plans for the new London Airport included water runways in a vast flying boat lake, and at Cowes on the Isle of Wight the mighty turbine-powered Princess was built and tested.

But it was not to be. Princess was stillborn and in terms of economy the landplane established its operational superiority. In odd corners of the world a few ageing flying boats linger on in service, and the Russian and Japanese navies still persevere with turbine-powered boats for anti-submarine patrol, but with the exception of those, and a few highly specialised craft like the Canadair CL 215 water-bomber, it seems that the flying boat story is ended.

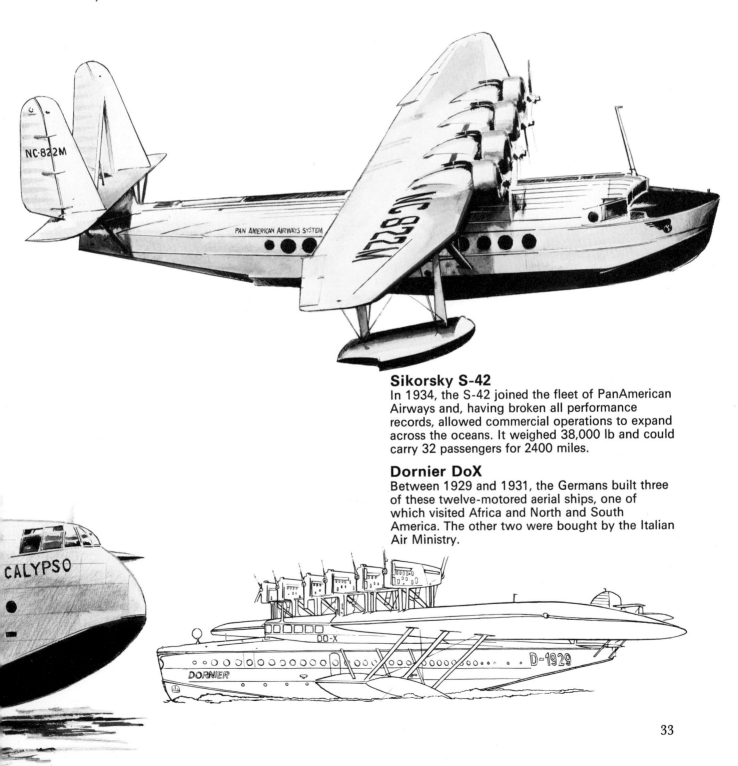

### Sikorsky S-42
In 1934, the S-42 joined the fleet of PanAmerican Airways and, having broken all performance records, allowed commercial operations to expand across the oceans. It weighed 38,000 lb and could carry 32 passengers for 2400 miles.

### Dornier DoX
Between 1929 and 1931, the Germans built three of these twelve-motored aerial ships, one of which visited Africa and North and South America. The other two were bought by the Italian Air Ministry.

## Boeing P-26A
The first monoplane fighter to go into production, the P-26 of 1932 was also the first all-metal machine to enter US Army service.

## Martin B-10
Aerodynamically speaking, the B-10 bridged the gap between the ancient biplanes and the sleek monoplanes with which the USAAF entered World War 2. This milestone in bomber design introduced new features, such as the retractable undercarriage, internal bomb stowage and a gun turret.

**Monoplanes**

### Hawker Hurricane
The prototype of the Hurricane took the air in 1935. Five years later, the design was proved one of the greatest of all time, when Hurricanes destroyed more enemy aircraft during the Battle of Britain than all other forms of defence combined.

# The Development of Advanced Airliners

Promising designs were delayed or halted by the outbreak of war in 1939. The desperate struggle for Europe ended all work on civil aircraft on that hemisphere, while development could continue for a year or two in the USA. When America entered the war at the end of 1941, airliners were converted to military transports.

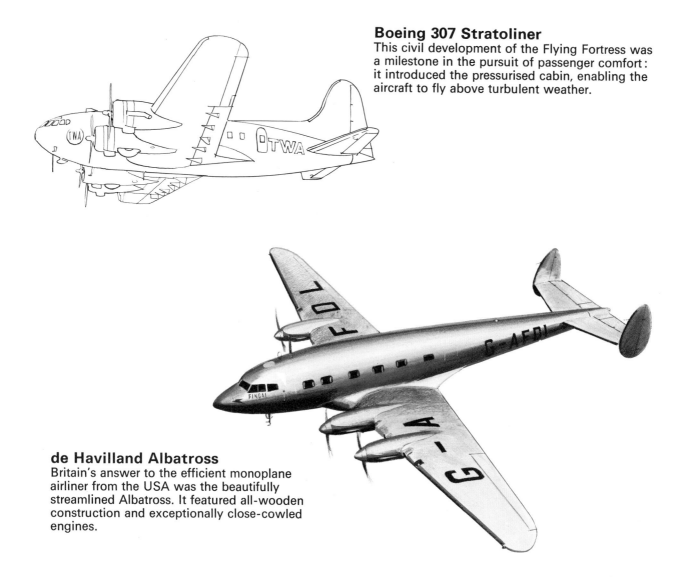

**Boeing 307 Stratoliner**
This civil development of the Flying Fortress was a milestone in the pursuit of passenger comfort: it introduced the pressurised cabin, enabling the aircraft to fly above turbulent weather.

**de Havilland Albatross**
Britain's answer to the efficient monoplane airliner from the USA was the beautifully streamlined Albatross. It featured all-wooden construction and exceptionally close-cowled engines.

# Fighters of the Battle of Britain

On a Bavarian airfield in September 1935, the roar of a Rolls Royce Kestrel signalled the end of the biplane era as the first Messerschmitt Bf 109 took to the air.

Others had pioneered stressed skin construction, cantilever wings, enclosed cockpits and retractable landing gear, but Messerschmitt combined all these features in the Me109. Six months later, on March 5, 1936, the Supermarine Spitfire followed its rival into the air. The two machines were remarkably similar in concept and performance, although the Spitfire's delicate lines contrasted markedly with the angular outline of the 109. Another low-wing single-seater, the Hawker Hurricane, had made its début on November 6, 1935, but it was an interim design with modern features—closed cockpit and retractable undercarriage—combined with the tubular metal and canvas of the biplane era. It is noteworthy that all three prototypes mounted Rolls-Royce engines, although production Me109s would be powered by Daimler-Benz.

As war clouds gathered, all three were ordered into mass production and in August 1940, 800 Me109s faced 700 Spitfires and Hurricanes across the English Channel. In addition the Luftwaffe had 1200 bombers, 230 twin-engined Me110 fighters and 250 Ju87 Stukas.

When battle was joined, the Me110s proved no match for Spitfire or Hurricane, and the Stuka, after terrible punishment, was withdrawn from battle and thereafter operated only where German fighters controlled the sky.

After attacks on Channel shipping, the Luftwaffe turned its attention to fighter bases and radar installations. The RAF, warned of impending attacks by radar and Observer Corps, scrambled its squadrons, where possible sending Spitfires to engage escorting fighters while Hurricanes attacked the bombers.

Spitfire and Messerschmitt 109 were evenly matched and often only luck or pilot skill decided the result of individual dogfights. Psychologically the British had the advantage of fighting over home territory. Damaged aircraft were never far from a friendly field and a shot-down pilot was often back in action within hours. In contrast, a Luftwaffe pilot who baled out or forced-landed faced imprisonment, while battle damage meant a long and hazardous haul over the unfriendly waters of the Channel.

While there was little to choose between the skill and courage of opposing pilots, the same could not be said of the opposing commanders.

On the British side, Air Chief Marshal Hugh C. T. Dowding, Commander-in-Chief of Fighter Command had, over a period of years, built up an integrated defence that combined sophisticated tracking and plotting systems with efficient control of fighters in the air. Against a numerically superior force, Dowding fought a campaign which ranks in British history with Nelson's victory at Trafalgar and the destruction of the Spanish Armada.

The German leadership, on the other hand, were guilty of the supreme folly of underrating the enemy. Their plan of attack was hastily formulated and based on intelligence which bore little or no resemblance to the facts. Commanders in the field were subject to interference by Hitler and Göring in their headquarters hundreds of miles from the battle. The classic example of such interference came at the end of August. On the 25th, an error by a German navigator resulted in bombs falling on civilian targets in east London—in contravention of a directive from Adolf Hitler.

That mistake was a turning point. Winston Churchill, against the advice of his cabinet, ordered the Royal Air Force to attack Berlin. The few bombers which found their target caused little damage but they made nonsense of Göring's boast that enemy bombers would never darken German skies.

In a fury, Hitler ordered the Luftwaffe against London—and at that critical moment in the battle, when Fighter Command was reeling from incessant attacks on its bases and installations, the pressure was suddenly eased.

German fighters now had to operate at ultimate range allowing only minutes of combat over the target, and bomber crews who had been told time and again that the RAF was finished now faced the fury of massed fighter squadrons on every side. On September 15, two attacks by vast formations of bombers and fighters were broken up and scattered across southern England. Fifty-eight aircraft and their crews failed to return and many more struggled home with engines blazing and crewmen dead or dying.

The raids would go on by day and night but to all intents and purposes the Battle of Britain ended on the evening of September 15, 1940 and its finish marked the beginning of the end for the Third Reich.

## Supermarine Spitfire

The most famous fighter of all, the Spitfire became a legend not only in its native Britain but in world history. With the Hurricane, it emerged victorious from the Battle of Britain. Here a 'Spit' shoots down a Dornier Do17 high flying photographic reconnaissance aircraft of the Luftwaffe. The Spitfire was developed and improved as the war went on, until no less than 22,742 had been built.

## Consolidated PBY 5A Catalina
One of the most reliable naval patrol bombers, the
Catalina was worked hard by the US Navy Marine
Corps, RAF Coastal Command and the Soviet Navy.
The wing floats folded to form the wing tips.
One version of this versatile flying boat was made
amphibious by the addition of a retractable
undercarriage.

## Vought-Sikorsky OS2U Kingfisher
An observation floatplane designed for the US Navy in 1939. The OS2U was the first monoplane to be catapulted from the decks of battleships and cruisers to spot gunfire. The long single float was a notable feature.

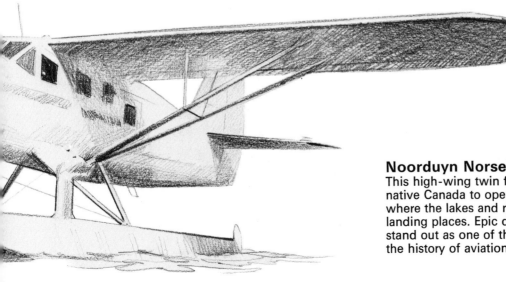

## Noorduyn Norseman
This high-wing twin floatplane was used in its native Canada to open up the distant bush country where the lakes and rivers offered the only possible landing places. Epic deeds by the 'bush pilots' stand out as one of the most exciting chapters in the history of aviation.

## Consolidated B-24 Liberator
Almost as famous as the B-17, and judged to be more efficient as a load carrier, the B-24 served with distinction an all fronts during World War 2. Used in great numbers in Europe the 'Lib' will be remembered for the low level assault on the Rumanian oil complex at Ploeşti.

## Boeing B-17 Flying Fortress
One of the most successful aircraft of World War 2, the Fortress first flew in 1935. Developed versions were used in massive numbers for the US high altitude daylight bombing assault on Hitler's Europe.

**The Daylight Bomber**

# The Daylight Bomber

The concept of precision daylight bombing was developed in 1920 by General 'Billy' Mitchell, who foresaw bomber formations capable of destroying industries and disrupting communications. Mitchell's theories antagonised the higher command and ended in court-martial, but within a decade the US Army Air Corps was formulating requirements which came to fruition in 1935 with the first flight of the Boeing XB-17.

The XB-17 earned the somewhat fanciful description 'Flying Fortress', but by the autumn of 1942 the production B-17 was a flying fortress in fact, and together with the B-24 Liberator, formed the heavy bomber arm of the US Eighth Air Force based in Britain.

Daylight bombing had already been tried and found wanting by the RAF and the Luftwaffe, both forces concluding that the day bomber could not survive in the face of determined fighter defence. After the Battle of Britain, Luftwaffe day bombing in the west was restricted to hit-and-run attacks by fighter bombers, while the RAF confined offensive daylight operations to fighter sweeps and short range bomber raids with massive fighter escort. Luftwaffe and RAF high commands were therefore watching the Eighth Air Force build-up with keen professional interest.

The first attack, by twelve B-17s escorted by RAF Spitfires, took place on August 17, 1942 against rail installations at Rouen. Damage was caused to rail workshops and rolling stock, and two Me109s were destroyed for the loss of two Spitfires. The B-17s all returned safely but this raid was not to be typical of the years to come and American bombers were to suffer savage losses as the Luftwaffe got the measure of their new opponents.

On August 17, 1943, first anniversary of the Rouen raid, a two-pronged attack was launched, with 147 Fortresses of the 4th Wing striking Messerschmitt factories at Regensburg and flying on to land in North Africa, while 1st Wing was to attack the Schweinfurt ball bearing works and return to England. The plan called for P-47 Thunderbolts to escort 4th Wing on part of the outward trip, the 1st Wing strike being timed to take advantage of German preoccupation with 4th Wing.

In the event, 4th Wing faced heavy attacks from FW190s, Me109s, Me110s and Ju88s. Seventeen B-17s were lost before the target was reached, but the attack was pressed home and production of Me262 jet fighters was disrupted. In all, 24 bombers failed to reach North Africa.

Meanwhile 1st Wing had been delayed by fog and German fighters had time to re-arm. Two hundred and thirty B-17s set out for Schweinfurt with P-47s escorting to the German frontier. The Luftwaffe reacted with 200 FW190s and Me109s and fighting reached a hitherto unmatched ferocity. Again the target was hard hit but 36 bombers were lost with 370 airmen missing and many more dead and wounded.

In all, 60 B-17s were lost against 25 German fighters destroyed. Such losses would have been unsupportable over a long period, but a new factor dramatically affected the daylight air war. The expendable fuel tank, mass-produced in British factories, would allow the P-47s to escort their charges deep into Germany.

On September 27, 1943, P-47s accompanied B-17s all the way to Emden and destroyed 21 German fighters for the loss of a single Thunderbolt. It was a turning point and although fighting in the next year would mount in intensity, the time was coming when B-17s and B-24s would roam at will in German skies.

The Eighth Air Force vindicated the protagonists of daylight bombing and in so doing they played a major part in the destruction of the German war machine.

# RAF Bomber Command

In direct contrast to the campaign of the United States Eighth Air Force, RAF Bomber Command directed almost all of its resources into night bombing. British bomber crews had learned the hard way over the Franco-German frontier and Heligoland Bight that the daylight bomber had little chance where the enemy had air superiority. In consequence, with few exceptions, British daylight operations were restricted first to fighter sweeps, then to hit-and-run attacks by Mosquitos which could almost match the opposing fighters in speed, and only much later to daylight medium and heavy bomber attacks with powerful fighter escorts.

A handful of obsolescent Wellingtons and Witleys could never have achieved more than nuisance value against German industry. But from the end of 1940 a new factor, the four-engined heavy bomber, began to come into play. First the Stirling, then the Halifax and Lancaster—powerful, heavily-armed bombers capable of carrying heavy loads deep into Germany. And instead of a mere ten or twelve machines reaching the target, the attackers now came in hundreds.

In April 1942, nearly 500 bombers attacked the Heinkel works at Rostock and on May 30, a thousand machines—virtually every British bomber that could be coaxed into the air —attacked Cologne. The German night fighter organisation was being swamped.

At this point the RAF attempted a low-level daylight raid against a priority target at Augsburg with 12 unescorted Lancasters. The target was hard-hit but only five Lancs returned to base and Bomber Command was reinforced in its view that night bombing was the best strategy.

Although mass bombing attacks continued almost until the moment of the German surrender, the climax of destruction was reached in July 1943. On the night of the 24th, aided by a secret radar jamming device known as 'window', 791 heavy bombers raided Hamburg, losing only twelve of their number to the defences. On the next two days, USAF B-17s attacked in daylight, and on the 27th another 722 RAF heavies returned, followed by a further 699 on the night of the 29th. In four nights more than 3000 bombers dropping 9000 tons of high explosive pounded the city into rubble. Firebombs ignited the devastated city centre and Hamburg was swept by a storm of fire against which all human effort was powerless. By the first day of August 1943, the city had been gutted and more than 31,000 people had perished—only the atomic bomb could more effectively have wiped a major city from the face of the earth.

**Vickers Wellington**

## Handley Page Heyford
The RAF's last biplane heavy bomber spanned the years 1933-39. By comparison with the Mosquito, the great technological advances spurred on by war are dramatically demonstrated.

## Avro Lancaster
The mainstay of the RAF strategic night bombing force from 1942, the 'Lanc' was described by the officers who directed the offensive as the greatest single factor in the winning of World War 2.

## de Havilland Mosquito

Nearly eight thousand Mosquitoes were built. Of wooden construction and capable of speeds higher than most fighters of its day, it was able to carry a 4000 lb bomb to Berlin from the United Kingdom. This extremely versatile aircraft also excelled as a day and night fighter and in reconnaissance.

# Operation Barbarossa—and the retreat from Moscow

In the first light of dawn on June 22, 1941, the Luftwaffe struck the first blow of Operation Barbarossa. Hand-picked crews dived their Ju88s and He111s from high altitude onto the forward bases of the Soviet Air Fleet. Three bombers allocated to each airfield scattered hundreds of fragmentation bombs among parade-ground rows of fighters and Stormoviks. Surprise was complete and before the Russians could recover from the initial confusion, the Luftwaffe returned in full strength to complete the destruction. Not a single Russian fighter opposed the onslaught and once again the Stukas reigned supreme—what it had failed to do over the coast of Britain it achieved in full measure over the Russian countryside. In one day, a total of 1811 Soviet aircraft were destroyed for the loss of thirty-five German machines.

As the first bombs were falling at daybreak, massed German tanks rolled across the frontier. Deprived of air support and subjected to incessant Stuka attack, the Russian armies were routed. As days lengthened into weeks it seemed that the Germans were indeed in-invincible—massive Soviet reinforcements failed to do more than slow the enemy's advance and, by November 1941, the German armoured division were poised for the final onslaught against Moscow.

But just as Hitler had underestimated the British in 1940, so he failed to appreciate the enormous resources of the Soviet Union. After the initial devastation of June 22, the Red Air Fleet fought back and despite appalling losses, the Il-2 Stormoviks and Pe-3 light bombers inflicted heavy losses on German armour. The bravery of the Russian pilots won the grudging admiration of their adversaries—however many were destroyed by German fighters and anti-aircraft guns, more always came to take their places. Russian aircraft factories, safe beyond the range of He111s and Ju88s, quadrupled their output, producing a total of 15,735 aircraft of all types in 1941. Once again the ghost of General Wever (see page 60) had returned to haunt the Luftwaffe—with his Urals bomber, the Russian aircraft industry could have been smashed—without it, the Luftwaffe was impotent and the German on-slaught against Russia was doomed to failure.

German tanks ground to a halt within sight of Moscow and, on December 5, the Russians launched their counter attack. After fierce fighting, the German line began to crack, and then the bitter winter set in. Operation Barbarossa had been planned as a blitzkreig and little thought had been given to the problems of a campaign in the snows of Russia. Fresh Russian armies, well equipped to face the extremes of winter, now swept the Germans westward. By February 1942, the German 10th army corps and elements of the 11th corps had been surrounded at Demyansk.

To the Luftwaffe now fell the duty of supplying a hundred thousand soldiers. Ju52 transports were withdrawn from other fronts—some squadrons flew straight from the sun scorched sands of the western desert to a nightmare world where rubber hoses would shatter like glass and a mechanic, spanner in hand, could quite literally become frozen to an engine.

Despite the worst the weather and the Russians could throw against them, the Luftwaffe continued an airlift for three months, carrying a daily average of 276 tons of supplies. They flew in 15,446 replacement troops and evacuated 22,093 wounded men. Their losses totalled 265 aircraft but they succeeded and by May the beleaguered troops had been relieved.

In 1942 the fortunes of war fluctuated but as the year drew to its close the stage was being set for the greatest military disaster of all times. In the autumn General Friedrich von Paulus' 6th Army was on the attack, battling street by street through the industrial city of Stalingrad. More than eighty per cent of the city was in German hands, but once again the Russian counter attack coincided with the onset of winter. The German advance was halted but worse was to follow. Hitler's personal orders to von Paulus allowed no retreat and the 6th Army stood and fought in the city while Russian armour advanced rapidly on either side. By November 22, the pincers had closed and a quarter of a million men were encircled.

The Luftwaffe's success in supplying the 10th and 11th army corps at Demyansk was an unfortunate precedent. This time the Russians were sweeping routed German armour before them and there was little chance that Stalingrad could ever be relieved.

Far from the front line, Göring had assured Hitler that his Luftwaffe could save the 6th Army and German airmen made a magnificent effort to make good his boast. The task was, however, insuperable: although at one stage 750 tons of supplies a day were being delivered against a minimum requirement of 600 tons, the daily average in fact was little more than 100 tons. And all the time the Russians grew stronger. Much improved fighters, the Mig 3 and Lagg 3, and new ground attack aircraft were flowing from the factories in thousands and the Luftwaffe no longer had undisputed control of the sky.

On December 24, the first Russian shells fell on Tazinskaya airfield, main base for the airlift transports, and a few days later the second transport field at Morosovskaya was over-run by Russian tanks.

The airlift continued under even greater difficulties from a base sixty miles from Stalingrad. In desperation the Luftwaffe threw in eighteen FW200 Condors withdrawn from the Atlantic coast and the disastrously unsuccessful He 177 long range bomber. But it was hopeless—by the end of January the Luftwaffe had lost 490 transports with their crews and despite their efforts the 6th Army was without food or ammunition. On February 2, 1943, von Paulus ordered his men to put down their arms.

The German army lost a quarter of a million of its finest fighting men in the ruins of Stalingrad—a shattering defeat from which it never recovered. There were to be a few local successes in 1943, but the invincible army which had smashed all opposition in Operation Barbarossa and which, within six months, had stood at the gates of Moscow was now demoralized, outgunned and outgeneralled. The long retreat from Moscow would end only in the ruins of Berlin.

**Pe2**
The Soviet Petlyakov Pe2 reconnaissance and dive bomber, based on the French Potez 63, was one of the best light bombers of World War 2.

# RAF Coastal Defence

## Avro Anson

Significant in RAF history, the Anson was the first monoplane to join the squadrons and also first to feature retractable landing gear. Entering service in 1936, it was finally retired in 1968.

## Lockheed Hudson

The Hudson was the first American-built aircraft to go on operations with the RAF in World War 2, when it replaced the Anson and distinguished itself on coastal patrol work.

## Bristol Beaufighter

The 'Beau' carried airborne radar into the RAF's battle against the night bomber, and served as a long-range strike fighter with Coastal Command. Shown here is a Royal Australian Air Force Beaufighter, which became known to the Japanese as 'Whispering Death'.

# American Tactical Bombers

**Martin B-26 Marauder**
A Marauder of the US Ninth Air Force based in Britain, 1944.

**Douglas A-20 Boston**
One of the best-known American aircraft used by the RAF and the first in service to use a tricycle undercarriage.

**North American B-25 Mitchell**
Carried a bomb load of 3000 lb at 275 mph over a range of 1350 miles.

# By Air into Battle

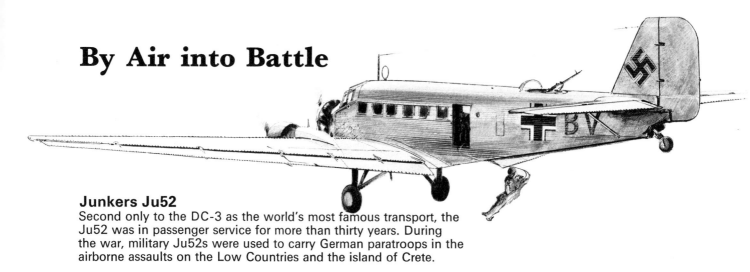

## Junkers Ju52

Second only to the DC-3 as the world's most famous transport, the Ju52 was in passenger service for more than thirty years. During the war, military Ju52s were used to carry German paratroops in the airborne assaults on the Low Countries and the island of Crete.

To the high command of the German armed forces must go the credit for evolving the methods of conveying fighting men into battle by air. There are three distinct methods of airborne assault: by transport-aircraft landing at an airfield newly siezed from the enemy; by parachuting into enemy-held territory; by glider into enemy-held territory. All three systems were developed in Germany in the 1930s and all three were employed with varying degrees of success in the blitzkriegs across Norway, France, Belgium and Holland.

One particularly memorable operation concerned the capture of the vital Oslo-Fornebu airfield close to the Norwegian capital. The plan called for two companies of paratroops to sieze and hold the field under covering fire from eight Messerschmitt 110s. The field would then be secured by troops landed from Ju52s, and the covering Me110s, by then low on fuel, would land at the newly-captured field.

The plan misfired. The paratroop transports ran into fog and low cloud and turned back after two machines had crashed into mountains. Over Fornebu, the Me110s were battling with Norwegian Gladiators, unaware that the paratroops had returned to Germany. Two Gladiators had crashed in flames on the airfield and two Messerschmitts had also been shot down, when the first of the troop-carrying Ju52s arrived on the scene. Its pilot, confident that the airfield must already be in the hands of German paratroops, came into land and ran into heavy Norwegian fire. With heavy damage and casualties, he managed to stagger back into the air. Above him, the Me110s were almost out of fuel and their leader First Lt Hansen decided that if the army couldn't take Fornebu then the Luftwaffe would have to do it for them. One by one, the fighters touched down while Hansen gave covering fire and then landed himself. They unshipped the rear cockpit machine guns and, joining forces with their colleagues shot down earlier, they took control of the airfield without another shot being fired. As the Messerschmitts had landed, a second Ju52 appeared over the airfield boundary and landed, soon followed by the remainder of the troop carriers, but the engagement had already been won.

The troop-carrying glider, conceived in the last years of peace, enjoyed a few brief moments of glory in action and then passed into history soon after the end of the World War 2. Its first battle was the capture of the reputedly impregnable Belgian fortress of Eben Emael. At 0310 hours on May 10, 1940 the 7th Belgian Infantry Division was at action stations inside the fortress. Black shadows suddenly swooped down from the eastern sky, landing amid anti-aircraft guns which scarcely had time to open fire. Ten DFS 230 gliders disgorged seventy-five shock troops with two and a half tons of explosive. Small demolition charges were flung through gun apertures and in minutes the fort's heavy weapons had been silenced. The garrison fought on gallantly but their position was hopeless and at 1315 hours Eben Emael surrendered—a key fortress captured by a handful of glider troops for the loss of six dead and twenty wounded.

The biggest airborne operation mounted by the Germans, the invasion of Crete on May 20, 1941, was also their last. It involved some 500 Ju52s towing gliders, dropping paratroops and, when an airfield had been secured, landing re-inforcements. The operation succeeded but only at the cost of appalling losses—3600 soldiers and 320 airmen died. In one drop of 600 men, 400 died before they could reach their weapon packs. Aircraft losses were also crippling; two hundred Ju52s were destroyed, in addition to at least as many fighters and bombers. The glider and paratroop units were reformed after the battle of Crete but they were never again used in a major action.

In June 1940, Winston Churchill ordered his Chief of Staff to institute a corps of at least 5000 parachute troops. In addition, a glider pilot regiment was created and with it the transport aircraft and gliders to carry the fighting men into action. Large-scale operations commenced on November 8, 1942, with the landings in French North Africa. From that point on, the 'Red Devils', as the Parachute Brigade came to be known, together with their airborne allies, spearheaded the victories in North Africa, Sicily, and Italy. On D-Day, more than 17,000 allied airborne troops parachuted and glided into Normandy, causing chaos far beyond the perimeters of the seaborne landings and preventing reinforcement of the German coastal defences.

Later, an even greater airborne operation was to be mounted to capture the crossings of the Rivers Maas, Waal and the lower Rhine—the bridges at Gave, Nijmegen and Arnhem. This operation opened up the high road into the Third Reich—the bridges at Grave and Nijmegen were captured by the American 101st and 82nd Airborne Divisions and held until relieved by the advancing Second Army. Arnhem was the objective of the British 1st Air-borne Division, aided by the 1st Polish Parachute Brigade. The bridge was seized and held by them for three days, until their food and ammunition had given out and scarcely a man remained unwounded. No relief came, despite heroic efforts by the Second Army, and at last the Germans recaptured the bridge.

Today, paratroops continue to play a vital part in military planning, but the troop-carrying glider did not long survive the close of World War 2. Despite some brilliant successes, it was always a cumbersome and risky means of journeying into battle, and in modern warfare its place has been taken by the troop-carrying helicopter.

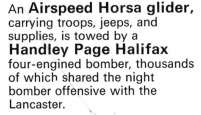

An **Airspeed Horsa glider,** carrying troops, jeeps, and supplies, is towed by a **Handley Page Halifax** four-engined bomber, thousands of which shared the night bomber offensive with the Lancaster.

**General Aircraft Hamilcar**
The seven-ton Tetrarch tank carried into battle by this large glider gave the Germans one of their biggest surprises when the Allies landed in France in June, 1944.

**North American P-51 Mustang**
The most famous American fighter of World War 2 (16,000 built), powered by the British-designed, Packard-built Rolls Royce Merlin, which gave superb performance leading to versatility of rôles from high altitude, long-range bomber escort to low-level ground attack fighter-bomber and photo recce. Served with USAAF and RAF. Still in use by South African Air Force in Korea in the early 1950s.

## Curtis P-40 Kittyhawk

Short range interceptor fighter seen in RAF colours over North Africa, 1942, where it was a fighter bomber. Known in US service as the Warhawk, it served in several Commonwealth Air Forces and with the Russians.

## Republic P-47 Thunderbolt

An outstandingly successful fighter of extremely rugged construction, used as a long-range bomber escort and also for low level ground attack duties with a useful load of bombs and rockets, This seven-ton heavyweight endeared itself to pilots and was affectionately known as the 'Jug' (short for Juggernaut). Used by the US in Europe and Pacific and the RAF in Burma.

# Three American Fighters

The P-40 was a direct descendant of the Curtiss Model 75 Hawk—most famous of all the pre-war American fighters. When the Hawk first took shape on the drawing boards of the Curtiss-Wright Airplane Division, the Me109, Spitfire and Hurricane were being formulated on the other side of the Atlantic.

As the P-36, the Hawk served with distinction on many fronts, but it was the P-40 which won fame in battle. In its various versions it was known as Tomahawk, Kittyhawk and Warhawk, and although somewhat slower than its contemporaries, it made up in agility for what it lacked in speed and firepower. P-40 is remembered with affection by the men who flew her—the American volunteers of the Tiger Squadron in China, the RAF pilots of the desert air force, the defenders of the Aleutians and the men of the Red Air Fleet.

The story of the P-51 began with an RAF order to North America for a version of their model NA-73, to be known as the Mustang Mk1. Powered by a 1000 hp Allison engine, this machine had a disappointing rate of climb and a poor performance at altitude. In British service the Mustang was soon relegated to army co-operation duties, but trials were carried out on an airframe re-engined with a 1520 hp Packard/Rolls Merlin, and this proved to be a truly potent combination. Top speed was now 440 mph at 35,000 feet, and increased internal fuel tanks plus external tankage gave the new machine, known as P-51B by the USAAF, sufficient range to escort British-based American bombers all the way to Berlin and back.

Another fighter which had a dramatic impact on the European air war was the P-47 Thunderbolt. This massive machine stemmed from two pre-war fighters designed by Major Seversky—the P-35 and the P-43 Lancer. Neither of its ancestors was popular with USAAF flyers, and when the Thunderbolt first arrived at British bases in January 1943, its prodigious weight and bulk drew critical comment from pilots accustomed to Spitfires and Kitty hawks.

Introduction into service was marred by engine and structual failures, but by the summer of 1943 most of the problems have been solved and P-47 pilots had gained confidence in their huge mounts. German pilots were also treating the Thunderbolt with growing respect—and with good reason: on July 30, 1943 Major Eugene Roberts, flying a P-47, became the first American pilot to be credited with three victories—two Fw190s and a Me109—on a single mission. An even more dramatic illustration of the Thunderbolt's prowess occurred on August 16, when P-47s escorting B-17s over France shot down eighteen German fighters for the loss of a single P-47. All the B-17s involved in that mission returned safely to their British bases.

# Battle for Midway

By the end of May 1942 the largest fleet in naval history had assembled in Japan's Inland Sea: two hundred ships including eleven battleships, eight carriers, twenty-two cruisers, sixty-five destroyers and twenty submarines. Against this armada the United States had three carriers, including the only partially repaired *Yorktown*, 8 cruisers and 14 destroyers.

Yamamoto had ordered his submarines to form a cordon west of Pearl Harbor to give warning of the approach of American carriers. These submarines were due on station by May 31, but here luck deserted the Japanese for the first time. Admiral Nimitz, Commander-in-Chief of the US Pacific Fleet, had been warned by naval codebreakers of Yamamoto's intentions and had already ordered his ships to sea. The carriers *Enterprise* and *Hornet* had sailed safely through the cordon line on May 29, and *Yorktown*, limping on reduced power, slipped through unseen in the early hours of the 30th.

The battle opened at 05.00 hours on June 3, when a diversionary attack hit Dutch Harbor in the Aleutians. Nimitz was not misled, however, as his intelligence units had already pinpointed Midway as the Japanese target. His reconnaissance aircraft were already scouring the ocean to the west of Midway for the enemy's First Carrier Striking Force under the command of Admiral Nagumo. First contact with Japanese ships came at 09.00 hours, when a PBY flying boat sighted the transports and escorts of the Midway Occupation Force. Nimitz realized that these were not Nagumo's ships, but nine B-17s and four PBYs were despatched to make what proved to be a relatively ineffectual attack.

Nagumo launched his bombers against Midway at 04.54 hours on June 4. At 05.30 his flagship *Akagi*, accompanied by the carriers *Kaga*, *Soryu* and *Hiryu*, was spotted by a patrolling PBY, and a few minutes later a second PBY saw and reported the Japanese formations *en route* for Midway. The bombers hit the atoll at 06.30, and escorting Zeros routed the obsolete Buffalo fighters sent against them, but by now Nimitz knew the approximate location of Nagumo's carriers. Nagumo, on the other hand, because of inadequate reconnaissance and faulty radio equipment, was still unaware that a powerful American carrier force was within three hundred miles. Believing himself safe from attack by carrier bombers he ordered a second strike against Midway. At this point the Japanese carriers were attacked by land-based Avengers and B-17s. No damage was caused and seven of the ten attacking bombers were destroyed, but the second strike on Midway was delayed.

Nagumo decided to continue with the Midway raid and further ordered that torpedo bombers, held as a defence against enemy surface ships, should be re-armed with bombs. This caused some confusion aboard *Akagi* and *Kaga* which each had eighteen torpedo bombers ready to launch. As the re-arming began Nagumo received the first intimation that American surface units were within striking range. There was as yet no indication that the enemy fleet included a carrier, but to Nagumo's problems were now added an attack by sixteen Midway-based Dauntless dive bombers. Eight were destroyed by Zeros and the others driven off. They were followed by fifteen B-17s bombing from 20,000 feet. The total effect of both raids was a near miss on *Akagi*, but again the second strike had been delayed. And now came confirmation that the American ships included a carrier.

Aircraft returning from the first Midway raid were landed on an Yamamoto was informed that the striking force was making all speed to intercept the enemy ships. Under a protective screen of Zeros, bombs were unloaded and torpedos replaced. At 09.20 *Akagi* and *Kaga* were about to launch a torpedo strike when fifteen aircraft were spotted coming in at wave-top height. These were Devastators from the USS *Hornet* attacking without fighter escort. They were hit at once by patrolling Zeros and then by an inpenetrable wall of ships ack-ack. All were destroyed without scoring a hit, but once more the launching of Nagumo's bombers had been delayed. Then came Devastators from the *Enterprise* and they fared little better: no damage was inflicted on the Japanese ships, and only six of the forty-one attackers returned to the *Enterprise*. But the sacrifice of the Devastators drew the Zeros down to sea level, and no one aboard saw the Dauntless dive bombers falling from the sky until it was too late.

On *Akagi* the first Zero was lifting off when a bomb tore a huge hole in the flight deck. A second bomb destroyed the midship elevator and fire spread out of control through the ship. Piles of bombs left on deck and in the hangar exploded, and within minutes the mighty *Akagi* was a blazing hulk.

Nagumo transferred his flag to the cruiser *Nagara* and his remaining carrier *Hiryu* launched a strike against the *Yorktown* hitting her three times and putting her out of the battle.

At 17.00 the American pilots found their target and plummeted down out of the sun. The giant carrier twisted and turned, but her time had run out: four bombs tore into her flight deck and re-armed bombers ready for take-off burst into flames and exploded. As the Dauntless formations reformed and swung away to the west, *Hiryu* shuddered to a stop.

**Curtiss SB2C Helldiver**
This dive bomber played a distinguished part in the vital sea-battles in the Pacific War.

**Grumman TBM Avenger**
This three-seat bomber became famous in Naval service because of its ability to carry a twenty-two inch torpedo which wrought havoc among enemy shipping.

# US Navy Carrier-borne Aircraft

## Chance Vought F4U Corsair
By the summer of 1945, more than 10,000 Corsairs had been delivered to the US Navy, Marines and Royal Navy for use as both land and carrier-based fighters.

## Douglas SBD Dauntless
In service at the outbreak of war, the Dauntless dive bomber did more than any other aircraft to halt the Japanese advance in the Pacific.

# Birth of the Luftwaffe

When Adolf Hitler became Reich Chancellor in 1933 he entrusted to Hermann Göring, one-time leader of the famed Richthofen Geschwader, the task of creating a new German air force, to be known as the Luftwaffe. The matter was urgent, but Göring did not have to start completely from scratch. In 1922, Germany had signed the Treaty of Rapallo with the Soviet Union. This contained a secret clause giving Russia the benefit of German aviation research in return for the use of a Russian air force base and experimental centre to train future Luftwaffe aircrews and technicians.

The German aircraft industry had, for five years previously, devoted itself to the development of military aircraft in direct contravention of the Treaty of Versailles. As a result Heinkel was able, in the summer of 1933, to test fly the protoype He51. This fighter provided the backbone of the fledgling Luftwaffe, and on August 18, 1936 it was the first German aircraft to see service with the Spanish nationalist air force. In November of the same year, the German Condor Legion commenced operations alongside the nationalists. The Condor Legion was to provide a baptism of fire for the Luftwaffe's future aces and commanders— men such as Adolf Galland, Werner Mölders and Hugo Sperrle. It also provided a testing ground for the latest warplanes—the Heinkel 111, the Junkers 87 and, perhaps most important, the Messerschmitt 109.

Some of the lessons drawn from the experience in Spain were however misleading. The immunity of the Heinkel 111 medium bomber from the near-obsolete Russian fighters which opposed it bred a complacency in the Reichsluftfahrtministerium (RLM) that was to contribute in large measure to the attrition of Luftwaffe bomber groups in the Battle of Britain. Another misleading conclusion drawn from the Spanish air war related to the Junkers Ju87—the legendary 'Stuka'. The Ju87 was the brainchild of World War One ace Ernst Udet, who had flown with Göring in the Richthofen Geschwader. Udet, a playboy and sporting pilot in the early 1930s, became obsessed with the concept of the dive bomber. He saw and piloted the Curtiss Helldiver during a visit to the United States and he persuaded Göring to purchase two of these biplane dive bombers for Luftwaffe trials. Flight tests seemed to bear out Udet's enthusiasm and the RLM Technical Office issued specifications to Arado, Blohm und Voss, Heinkel and Junkers. The first prototype to fly was the Junkers 87, and despite early problems it was ordered into mass production as the standard Luftwaffe divebomber.

In 1936, an accident occurred which may have changed the course of history. The newly appointed Chief of General Staff, General Wever, was passionately committed to the development of a long-range heavy bomber. With Kesselring he formulated the specification of the so-called 'Urals bomber', which came to fruition in the Dornier 19—an aeroplane remarkable similar to the trio of heavy bombers then taking shape in Britain. But on June 3, 1936, General Walther Wever died in the crash of a Heinkel 'Blitz Bomber' at Dresden, and with him, fortunately for Britain, died the Urals bomber.

Now the pattern was set. The warplanes with which Germany would fight the first years of the Second World War were already under test or in production. The Me 109 and FW 190 for air superiority over the front; He11, Ju88, Do17 and 215 bombers for tactical targets—airfields, railheads, troop concentrations; and the Stuka for pin-point targets— bridges, dams, strong points. Göring had been charged with the creation of a tactical air force, and in this he succeeded brilliantly—the actions in Poland, Belgium, Holland, France and Norway demonstrated how specialized air support enabled German armoured columns to smash numerically superior allied forces.

Where Göring failed was in not foreseeing the inevitable war with Britain and the need for long-range heavy bombers and high performance escort fighters to protect them.

# German Secret Weapons

In the years 1935-1945, the German aircraft industry spearheaded an incredible advance in the science of aerodynamics. Weapons which would have been regarded as pure science fiction before the war were developed and brought into service—and but for unbelievable stupidity on the part of the Nazi leaders, might well have affected the outcome of the war.

A jet turbine was bench-tested by Heinkel in 1937 and air-tested in the spring of 1939. In August 1939 the Heinkel 178, the world's first purely jet-propelled aircraft, made a successful first flight, but the Luftwaffe high command was unconvinced of its merit and Heinkel was ordered to concentrate on more conventional projects. Messerschmitt faced similar disapproval in high places when design of their jet fighter was initiated in 1938. Design proceeded, sometimes with—but often without—official approval. At the end of 1943, when the aircraft, now designated Me262, was almost ready for production, Hitler personally decided that it should be used as a 'Blitzbomber' rather than as an interceptor. This instruction, together with power plant problems, delayed the Me262's introduction into service until June 1944, when an experimental unit destroyed two P-38 Lightnings and a Mosquito.

The Me262 was without doubt the most effective fighter to see action in World War Two. With a top speed of 540 mph, it was 100 mph faster than its speediest opponent and in concept it set the pattern of aerial warfare for the next two decades. In July 1944, the RAF introduced the first British jet fighter, the Gloster Meteor Mk I into service, but apart from action against the V-1 flying bomb it was never to fire its guns in combat.

The V-1 was another dramatic secret weapon—a pilotless jet-propelled bomber which flew to its target on automatic guidance. Once in the target area, the ram-jet engine cut out and the V-1 dived into the ground. Even more incredible was the V-2, the world's first space vehicle. Operating from bases in France, the V-2 was an unmanned rocket which carried a one-ton warhead to an altitude of fifty miles and then plunged onto its target 200 miles away. Re-entering the earth's atmosphere at several thousand miles an hour—many times the speed of sound—it gave no warning of approach and there was no possibility of defence.

Several manned rocket vehicles were developed in Germany during the war. The most famous of these, the Me163 Komet, began life in the Messerschmitt project office in 1938, but once again indifference in high places delayed service debut until the end of 1944. The Me163 had a maximum speed of just under 600 mph in level flight and could climb to 30,000 feet in 2·6 minutes.

Many other German developments, which were actually tested in the air, have since become standard aviation practice—the podded jet motor, swept back (or swept forward) wings, the ejector seat, vertical take-off, and the delta wing now familiar on many modern aircraft—including, of course, the Concorde.

Perhaps the most remarkable of all German advanced projects was variable geometry. This concept was embodied in the Messerschmitt P1101 jet fighter which was captured by the Americans before it could be tested. The prototype P1101 was shipped to Wright Field and became the basis of the Bell X-5 variable sweep aircraft of 1951. Today, twenty-seven years after the capture of the P1101, only one variable geometry machine, the F111, is actually in service. Others, including the Mirage G, the Tomcat and the Mikoyan 'Flogger', are under test, while America's new stategic bomber, the B-1A, will be the first heavy aircraft to incorporate variable sweep.

Back in Germany, the company which designed the P1101 is now part of a consortium producing the swing-wing Panavia 200—Europe's Multi-Role-Combat-Aircraft, ordered for service with both the West German Air Force and the RAF.

## Messerschmitt Bf109

Germany's equivalent of the Spitfire won fame on all fronts throughout World War 2, more than 33,000 being built between 1936 and 1945.

## Junkers Ju88

Claims have been made that the Ju88 was the most versatile aircraft of World War 2. It served from 1939 until 1945 as both fighter and bomber.

**Focke-Wulf Fw190**
Very fast and heavily armed, the Fw190 was the Luftwaffe's standard fighter bomber from 1941 onwards.

**Junkers Ju87**
Known as the 'Stuka', this dive bomber was remarkably effective against ground targets, but was at a disadvantage when met by fighter opposition.

# Superfortress—The bomber that ended the Pacific War

The B-29 Superfortress began life as a US Defence Department requirement in January 1940. Known then as the Hemisphere Defence Weapon, the specification called for heavy defensive armament, armour plate, self-sealing fuel tanks, a maximum bomb load of 16,000 lb and the ability to carry a 2000-lb load for 5000 miles.

Boeing responded with their model 345, and in August 1940 two prototypes were ordered under the designation XB-29. In May 1941 full-scale production was authorised, and on September 21, 1942, the first Superfortress took off on its maiden flight—less than three years before the explosion of the first atomic bomb over Hiroshima.

Development of the B-29 was not without problems, chief among these being a tendency for the 2000 hp eighteen cylinder-Wright Cyclone engines to burst into flames in flight. On February 18, 1943, test pilot Eddie Allen radioed Boeing tower that he was returning to base with an engine fire. Tragically, the bomber went out of control as it approached the field, and struck an office block killing the crew and nineteen office workers.

In a remarkably short space of time, however, the snags had been ironed out, and this most complicated of warplanes was declared ready for action. It had been decided that the B-29 would operate exclusively in the Pacific theatre and first deliveries to operational units took place in the second half of 1943.

To accommodate the B-29s of the 20th Air Force, construction of vast new bases began in India and China. Building these bases involved thousands of transport missions both by heavy transport aircraft and by the B-29s themselves, while on the ground tens of thousands of Chinese laboured around the clock with primitive tools and with their bare hands. On June 5, 1944 the first B-29 combat mission took off from an Indian base to bomb targets in Bangkok. Ten days later 20th Air Force B-29s hit Yawata, the first time American bombs had fallen on the Japanese mainland since General Doolittle's epic raid on Tokyo in 1942.

But bombing Japan from India or China involved long hauls with minimum bomb loads, and it was not until US forces captured the Marianas in June 1944 that the full impact of the B-29 began to be felt. Five bases were constructed at Guam, Tinian and Saipan and the first units of the 21st Bomber Command were operational in October 1944. The first strike against Tokyo from the Marianas came on November 24, when 111 Superforts set out to raid the Musashino engine factory.

The Musashino mission discovered bugs and gremlins in plenty, both in the aircraft and the organisation. Not surprisingly perhaps, as a mere four years had elapsed since Boeing started construction of the first prototype, but nevertheless a bitter disappointment for the men of the 21st. Only 24 B-29s of the original 111 actually reached their target, and their bombs caused little damage owing to high altitude winds which reduced the accuracy of the bomb sights.

**Boeing B-29 Superfortress**
The most highly developed bomber of its time played a decisive rôle in the final phase of the war with an all-out assault on Japanese industry. The B-29 'Enola Gay' dropped the world's first atomic bomb on Hiroshima on August 6, 1945.

In January 1945, General Curtis Le May, one-time 3rd Division Commander in Britain, took over command of the 21st and began an intensive review of B-29 operations to date. By March the results of that review were announced to apprehensive bomber crews—in future they would bomb at night from altitudes as low as 5000 feet. There was a grain of comfort, however. In February 1945 US Marines had landed in Iwo Jima, midway between the Marianas Group and the Japanese mainland. In future battle-damaged bombers would find a haven on Iwo, and before VJ Day 2400 B-29s were to make emergency landings there. Equally comforting was the knowledge that the 'little friends' of the 21st, the P-51 Mustangs, would now be based at Iwo Jima and be able to provide escort all the way out and back.

On March 9, 300 B-29s bombed Tokyo from low level and left fifteen square miles of the city centre gutted by fire. And that was only the beginning. In the coming months sixty-nine major cities were subjected to fire bomb and high explosive and left almost totally destroyed.

As the Japanese homelands shuddered under a never-ending bombardment, surface forces were closing an ever-tightening ring. In June the island of Okinawa fell to US Marines and allied forces had a base little more than 300 miles from Japanese soil. Plans were now finalised for the final assault against an army of more than 2,000,000, every man of which was determined to fight to the death for his Emperor and homeland. There were few illusions about the coming battle—in comparison the bloody battles of western Europe and Russia would seem mere skirmishes.

But the battle was never fought and many millions of people—soldiers, sailors, airmen and civilians, are alive today who otherwise must inevitably have died. On Monday August 6, 1945, a single missile fell from the bomb bay of a B-29 named Enola Gay and below, a matter of seconds later, the city of Hiroshima ceased to exist and 140,000 people were dead or dying.

Three days after the destruction of Hiroshima another B-29 named Bock's Car attacked its alternate target and Nagasaki became the second city of the atomic age. For reasons both meteorological and topographical the casualty rate and the destruction were less than at Hiroshima, but it was enough. The citizens of Hiroshima and Nagasaki may not have appreciated the distinction, but their suffering gave the Japanese leaders an opportunity to bring the war to an honourable conclusion. The courage and determination of the Japanese armed forces was not in question, but their qualities would be of no avail against so terrible a weapon.

On September 2, 1945, General MacArthur received Japan's envoys for the formal ceremony of surrender and the war which began with a massed bomber raid on Pearl Harbor had ended with a single Superfortress flying unchallenged in the skies of Japan.

## The Advent of Jet Propulsion

### Gloster E28/39
The first British jet-propelled aircraft to fly. It took off from Cranwell on May 15, 1941. Frank Whittle began his research in 1928 and the first engine ran in 1937.

### Heinkel He178
The world's first jet aircraft flew for the first time in Germany on August 24, 1939, piloted by Captain Warsitz.

### Bell P-58 Airacomet
America's first jet flew on October 1, 1942. The power plants were two US-built turbojets based on the British designs of Frank Whittle.

66

## Lockheed P-80 Shooting Star
The P-80 was the first operational jet to equip USAF fighter squadrons and was extensively used in the Korean War.

## de Havilland Vampire
The twin-boom single jet joined RAF Fighter Command in 1946.

## Gloster Meteor
The Meteor joined the squadrons in 1944 and became the only Allied jet to go into action in World War 2. In 1946, a Meteor raised the world speed record to 616 mph.

# The Development of the Airliner

Development of passenger aeroplanes between the wars progressed rapidly, but only a tiny proportion of travellers actually journeyed by air and few people believed that the airliner would ever rival the ocean liner as the normal means of travelling from one country to another.

The Second World War changed the picture completely. Military logistics demanded that men and equipment be moved speedily across oceans and mountain ranges regardless of cost. To meet this requirement the aircraft industry of the United States began the mass production of transport aircraft.

The basic allied transport was to be the Douglas DC3, variously known as Skytrain or Dakota. A twin-engined monoplane seating twenty-four passengers, it had seen service with a number of airlines in the late 1930s. In military guise more than 10,000 were built and it flew in every theatre of war, carrying men and supplies 'over the hump' into China, taking paratroops into action on D-Day. It towed gliders, dropped supplies to encircled armies and, fitted with skis, it serviced arctic outposts.

In addition to the DC3, two four-motor transports which had been flying in prototype before the war were also ordered into mass production. These were the Douglas DC4, later named Skymaster, and the Lockheed Constellation. Like the DC3 they were to see service on many fronts.

When war ended, many thousands of transport aircraft were declared surplus to requirements, together with masses of spares and ground support equipment. To this was added thousands of redundant aircrew eager to continue their flying careers. The scene was set for the explosive development of international air transport.

In the immediate post-war years the DC3 became the symbol of short range air travel. The skies around the airports seemed to be filled with Dakotas—and this was even true in Russia where a carbon-copy of the DC3 had been manufactured under the designation Li-2.

**Douglas C-54 Skymaster**
A C-54 landing at Berlin during the airlift, which carried nearly two and a half million tons of supplies into the blockaded city.

On long range international routes the DC4s and Constellations carried ever-increasing passengers loads and aircraft manufacturers began 'stretching' the basic designs to increase payload and improve economy. Douglas produced the DC6, a re-worked DC4 with longer fuselage, wider wing span and more powerful engines. The Constellation was succeeded by the Super Constellation, and in due course the DC6 was supplanted by the DC7; but still the call was for more passenger seats, greater comfort, longer range.

Boeing introduced the Stratocruiser, a development of the B-29, with a 'double-bubble' fuselage housing two decks and a spiral staircase. Britain also built airliners based on successful bomber designs. The Wellington sired the Viking and the Lancaster gave birth to the Tudor, but it was becoming clear that the piston engine had reached the peak of its development and must soon be superceded.

In the closing years of the war the pure jet gas turbine had begun to supplant the piston engine in military service, and that process had accelerated after the war, but the economics of the jet at that time were such that only military application were practicable. The solution of the problem seemed to be the prop-jet, a gas turbine with an extra stage driving a conventional airscrew. The first experimental airscrew turbine was the Rolls Royce Trent, which flew in September 1945 in a converted Meteor Mk I fighter. Soon design teams were at work on short, medium and long range airliners powered by an entirely new generation of air liners. Some of the short and medium range machines were to prove highly successful and continue in use to the day—the Viscount, Vanguard, Electra, Hawker Siddeley 748 and others, but the ultra-long-range prop-jet, typified by the Bristol Britannia, was overtaken by the unexpectedly rapid development of the pure jet engine.

In 1949 the world's first pure-jet airliner, the de Havilland Comet I took to the air, and by 1952 it was in service on medium range routes with BOAC. A series of disasters marred the Comet story and grounded the early versions, but by 1958 the Comet was back in service on BOAC's Atlantic route.

Today many Comets remain in service flying tourists on cheap 'packaged' holidays and a completely redesigned Comet 4, renamed Nimrod Mk I, is in large scale service with the Royal Air Force as a long-range maritime reconnaissance aircraft. Able to fly at high subsonic speed to its search area, it can cruise for long periods on two of its four Spey turbofan engines. Almost a quarter of a century after the first flight of the Comet I the basic design is making a come-back as the most efficient submarine hunter in the world—and it seems likely to remain in service for at least twenty years.

**Boeing Stratocruiser**
A double-decked derivative of the B-29 bomber.

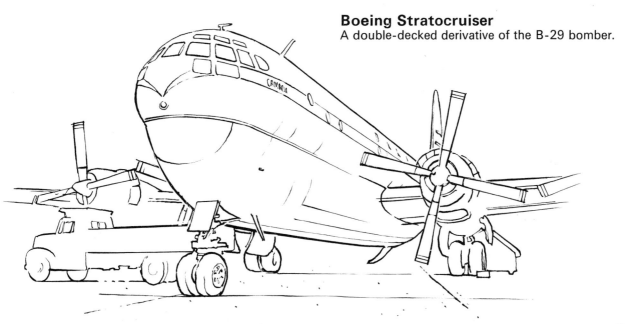

## The Turbine enters Service

### English Electric Canberra
The world's first jet bomber to enter service joined squadrons of the RAF in 1951 and is still in use today. The photo recce version depicted here won the 1953 London-New Zealand Air Race. As the B-57, the Canberra became the first British aircraft to be mass-produced in the USA. In 1957, a Canberra held the world height record of 70,310 feet.

### Vickers Viscount
The world's first turboprop airliner, the prototype of which flew in Britain in 1948, since when Viscounts have flown more than ten million hours on routes all over the world.

### de Havilland Comet
The world's first jet airliner made its maiden flight in England in July, 1949. Cruising at 490 mph, the Comet set entirely new standards of passenger comfort in high speed travel. On May 2, 1952, BOAC flew the first commercial jet service from London to Johannesburg.

# Korea—Sabre versus Mig

When North Korean ground forces swept across the 38th Parallel on June 25, 1950 they were setting the scene for the first jet-fighter confrontation.

In the early days of the campaign, when the communist forces all but swept the South Korean army and its handful of United States advisors into the sea, air activity was confined to ground attack by obsolete Yak-9s of the North Korean Air Force. Later, when southern forces were confined in a narrow perimeter around Pusan in the extreme south, United States Air Force F-80 Shooting Star jet fighters entered the battle, flying in from bases in Japan.

By August 1, the allied forces in the south had come under the command of the United Nations Organisation. The South Korean army had been re-organised and re-equipped, and the rapidly expanding US ground force was to be joined by the British 27th Brigade. As the United Nations force prepared to push north, F-80 Shooting Stars and F-84 Thunderjets were transferred to bases on the Korean mainland.

UNO air power quickly annihilated the remnants of the North Korean air force, and the jet fighters, backed up by B-29s of the Strategic Air Command, now turned their attention to ground targets, either in close support of ground forces, acting on instruction from mobile ground controllers, or striking enemy supply routes and installations far behind the lines. They were joined by bombers and fighters from British and American carrier groups operating off the Korean coast. In the bleak hills of Korea there was no place to hide: any North Korean Peoples Army unit that moved in daylight risked immediate attack with bombs, rockets and napalm and, even at night enemy road convoys were sought out and attacked by B-26 bombers on 'intruder' missions.

On September 15, 1950 United Nations forces effected a landing at Inchon on the west coast just south of the 38th Parallel. This led quickly to the re-capture of the southern capital Seoul and to the utter rout of the NKPA in South Korea. UN forces bottled up in the Pusan bridgehead now broke out and raced north, scattering the disorganised and demoralised enemy. Within days UN units crossed the 38th Parallel and swept on deep into North Korea.

At this point the Chinese Peoples Republic took a hand and allied forces increasingly came up against 'Chinese volunteers'—in fact regular units of the Chinese army backed by tanks and heavy artillery. By October it was estimated that there were not less than 20,000 Chinese troops operating south of the Yalu river—the border between China and Korea.

The inevitable Chinese counter-attack began on November 1, 1950, and for weeks the outcome of the fighting was in the balance. At one point units of the US 1st Marine Division reached the banks of the Yalu and were able to look into Manchuria, but eventually sheer weight of numbers prevailed and by early December UN forces were retreating.

And now a new factor entered the battle. As the Chinese pursued allied ground forces their convoys and installations were subjected to devasting attacks by both ground attack fighters and heavy bombers. To protect their extending lines of communication the Chinese air force joined the battle with the swept-wing Mig-15. The Russian-built jet fighters were powered with a copy of the British Rolls Royce Nene—an example of which had been presented to Stalin by the British Government in 1946. Operated from bases north of the Yalu—where they were safe from attack by UN bombers—the Mig-15 was a much superior machine to the elderly F80s and F84s, and in the face of Chinese air superiority the SAC heavy bombers could no longer operate in daylight.

At this critical stage the US 4th Fighter Interceptor Wing arrived in Korea. The 4th were equipped with the North American F-86 Sabre—the first swept-wing fighter to see service with a western air force. The stage was now set for the first aerial battles of the jet age.

The first clash came on December 17, when a flight of Sabres destroyed a Mig without loss to themselves, the three other Migs involved racing for safety across the Yalu. Two days later another flight of four Sabres met up with six Migs which made a head-on attack *without firing* and then headed for the border. Other early encounters were equally inconclusive, but on the morning of December 22, eight Sabres were bounced by four Migs at 40,000 feet and one Sabre was destroyed without the US pilots having a chance to fire a shot.

To the Americans it now ceased to be a game, and eight angry men took off at 15.25 to seek revenge. They found a formation of fifteen Migs and in short but furious battle destroyed six without loss. For a while the Chinese pilots seemed reluctant to tangle with the Sabres and the latter were able to concentrate on ground targets in support of the still retreating UN forces. In this period the Chinese made determined attempts to build fighter bases south of the Yalu river, but heavy bombers of the Strategic Air Command destroyed the installations as soon as they were completed. After three months of fruitless effort the Chinese abandoned the project.

The F-86s were now based at Suwon just south of Seoul and only a few minutes flying time from the front line. The Chinese advance was halted at the end of January 1951, and there followed a period of some two and a half years in which the front line remained relatively static while the aerial war over North Korea increased in intensity and the 100-mile-wide strip bordering the south bank of the Yalu became known as 'Mig Alley'.

In the first half of 1951, the decisive factor had been the inexperience of the Chinese fighter pilots. Although a number of B-29s were destroyed or damaged by opposing fighters in that period, only one Sabre had been lost to enemy action—and that had been destroyed on the ground in the course of an attack by an ancient PO-2 biplane which hedge-hopped over Suwon in the early hours of June 17. The PO-2 dropped two 25lb fragmentation bombs which wrecked one machine and badly damaged four others.

By July 1951 some of the Chinese pilots, led by Russian instructors, had gained sufficient confidence and experience to challenge the Sabres, and although the balance of aircraft destroyed remained very heavily weighted in favour of the Americans, Sabre losses in combat began to mount.

It had been estimated that in the second half of 1951 there were some 700 Mig-15s based in Manchuria compared to a total of 150 Korean-based Sabres. As previously noted, however, the US pilots were for the most part veterans of the Second World War, whereas most of their opponents were not long out of flying school. The result on occasions was a near fantasy situation where a hundred or more Mig-15s would flash and weave like a shoal of silver fish in the deep blue of the stratosphere watching the Sabre formations far below. Periodically, as their pupils looked on in admiration, Russian instructors and experienced Chinese fighter leaders would plunge down and seek battle. Mig Alley had become an operational flying school for the Chinese air force.

In July 1951 truce talks began but apart from a temporary lull in Mig sorties, the talks had little effect on the war in the air. Attacks continued on North Korean targets, but insupportable losses of heavy bombers forced the abandonment of daylight bombing. On November 2nd the one hundredth Mig was claimed by Lt Col Jones and First Lt Pincoski flying F-86s, and in the same month thirty-one Sabres attacked a formation of twelve Tu-2 bombers escorted by sixteen Lagg-9 piston engined fighters and sixteen Mig-15s. Eight Tu-2s, three Laggs and a Mig were destroyed for two Sabres damaged. The North Koreans never again attempted to use bombers against UN forces.

The war dragged on until July 27, 1953, and the Sabre versus Mig contest continued to the bitter end. Losses in combat were more than ten to one in favour of the US pilots with a final tally of 792 Migs destroyed for the loss of 78 F-86s. There can be little doubt that the F-86 Sabre, by containing the threat posed by a final total of well over 1000 Mig-15s, and by maintaining air superiority over the front line and over the greater part of North Korea, prevented numerically superior Chinese ground forces from driving UN forces from their positions on the 38th Parallel.

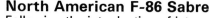

## North American F-86 Sabre

Following the introduction of jet propulsion, the
next technical improvement to fighter aircraft was
the incorporation of the swept-back wing, which
allowed the Sabre to approach the speed of sound.

## Mig-15

Russian-built Mig-15s had a better performance than any USAF machine when jets met in combat for the first time over Korea in 1951. The Mig owed its qualities largely to German aerodynamics and a basically British engine.

## Republic F-84 Thunderjet

In Korea, the F-84 proved ideal for ground attack on bridges, railways, dams and power-stations.

**North American X-15**
First to exceed Mach 6·7 and fly over 67 miles high

# Post-war Technology

Fighter development in World War 2 had seen maximum speeds rise to around 600 mph, and pilots and designers were becoming aware of a new aerodynamic phenomenon. The symptoms were violent buffetting of the airframe and sometimes a reversal of the normal effects of the control surfaces. The men whose job it was to overcome the problem called it 'compressibility'—the popular press called it the 'sound barrier'—and many authoritative articles appeared in technical journals, proving that this was one obstacle that science would not be able to surmount.

Events seemed to prove the writers correct. In 1946, the British government cancelled the Miles 1000 supersonic research aircraft on the grounds that pilots should not be asked to fly at such speeds. That decision not only put Britain out of the supersonic race but also crippled the development of British fighter aircraft. Early in the Korean war, RAF squadrons flying obsolete Meteors had to be withdrawn from battle because they were no match for the Russian Mig15—a fighter powered by a copy of the British Nene engine.

Some British companies pressed on with supersonic research on 'shoestring' budgets. The de Havilland designers developed the DH-108 tailless machine from the wartime Vampire jet fighter, but although it achieved higher speeds than any contemporary British aircraft, the trials ended in disaster when the machine broke up, killing the pilot Geoffrey de Havilland.

In America, the Bell Company produced the X-1 to an order from the US government. A missile-like craft with short-span unswept wings, it carried fuel sufficient for only a few minutes of powered flight and had to be launched from a B-29 'mother ship' at a height of 30,000 feet. In flight after flight, the pilot 'Chuck' Yeager approached closer and closer to the sound barrier—and with each speed increase the buffeting became more severe. Then on October 14, 1947, he opened the throttle wide and felt the buffeting increase until it seemed that he must lose control—but instead the rough ride ended abruptly and he was soaring smoothly through the deep blue of the stratosphere faster than any man had ever travelled before. The sound barrier had been broken.

Modified versions of the X-1 went on to achieve speeds of 1650 mph and other X craft followed to explore the new realm of supersonic flight, the ultimate development in the series being the X-15. This machine was launched from a B-52 mother ship and on its first powered flight in 1959 reached twice the speed of sound. Within a year, it was flying at 2000 mph and in 1962 an X-15 attained speeds greater than 4000 mph and climbed sixty miles above the earth's surface. thereby qualifying its pilot for astronauts 'wings'.

The lessons of high-speed research were applied, less spectacularly, to service aeroplanes. 'Trans-sonic' machines such as the Sabre, Hunter, Javelin and Vixen were able to reach and pass the speed of sound in a shallow dive while retaining good handling and fighting characteristics. The Hunter in particular proved to be a 'pilot's aircraft'—so popular, in fact, that it is still used as a yardstick when evaluating the flying characteristics of a new type. The Hunter first saw service with the RAF in 1954 and although it is now outclassed in the air combat role, it remains in service in many countries as a potent ground-attack aircraft.

The next step forward in military aviation was a fighter that could not only slip through the sound barrier in a dive but which could sustain supersonic speed for long periods. First of the new generation was the North American F-100 Super Sabre which had a maximum speed of 924 mph at 36,000 feet. With its four 20mm cannon and up to 7500 lb of bombs and rockets, the F-100 was a formidable weapon, but it was in fact only an interim type which pointed the way to 1500 mph fighter bombers capable of lifting up to eight tons of bombs and rockets.

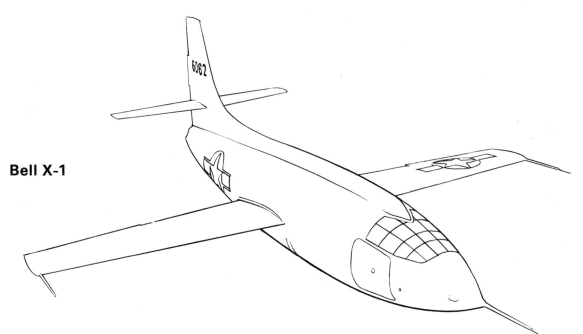

**Bell X-1**

# Fighters of the 'Cold War'

## Gloster Javelin
All-weather night fighter with distinctive delta-shaped wing, this large two-seater with comprehensive radar was armed with Firestreak air-to-air missiles. More than 230 Javelins flew with the RAF, commencing in 1956.

## Hawker Hunter
The Hunter was conceived in Britain as an interceptor fighter and later distinguished itself as a ground-attack aircraft. Its fine flying characteristics have made it popular with pilots in numerous air forces.

## North American F-100 Super Sabre
An advanced single-seat interceptor and
fighter-bomber derived from the Sabre, the F-100
first flew in 1953, and in the same year gained the
world's air speed record at 755 mph.

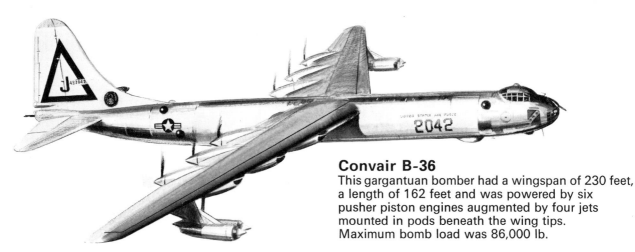

### Convair B-36
This gargantuan bomber had a wingspan of 230 feet, a length of 162 feet and was powered by six pusher piston engines augmented by four jets mounted in pods beneath the wing tips. Maximum bomb load was 86,000 lb.

# Nuclear Deterrent

When the shooting war ended in 1945, the 'Cold War' was not long in starting. Uneasy alliances forged in the heat of global conflict soon shattered in the political struggle for Europe, and what Churchill described as an 'Iron Curtain' descended, dividing East from West along the Lübeck-Trieste line.

In those first uneasy years following VE day, peace was maintained by the deterrent effect of American nuclear weapons carried in B-29s of the Strategic Air Command. There was, however, very little hope that the secret of atomic weapons would remain a monopoly of the West and in due course the Russians exploded first an atomic bomb and later the far more powerful hydrogen bomb. The 'great deterrent' had become a delicate balance of terror with each side recognising that any attack would lead inevitably to total mutual destruction.

The B-29s of SAC gave place to the B-36, a 230-feet-span giant with six 'pusher' propellers augmented in later marks by four turbo-jets. A B-36 in flight was an impressive sight, and the noise and vibration of its ten engines often announced its approach long before it came in sight.

On the Russian side a 'carbon copy' of the B-29, based on Superfortresses which had forced landed in Russian territory during 1945, was brought into service as the Tu-4, and for the first time the United States mainland was threatened by a long range bomber fleet. Ironically both the bombers and their atomic warloads were based on original American designs.

Britain also joined the 'nuclear club', and the piston engined bomber began to be phased out. In SAC service the B-36 gave way to the B-47 Stratojet (illustrated on pages 84-85),

### Boeing B-52 Stratofortress
Jet powered successor to the B-36, the B-52 was phased into the Strategic Air Command in 1955, and is still the backbone of the USAF's nuclear striking force. In 1957, three B-52s circled the earth non-stop in forty-five hours.

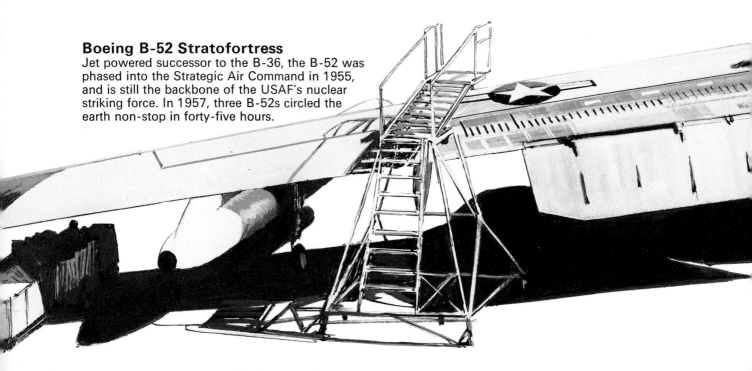

a six-engined swept-wing bomber with an operational radius of 1600 miles and a maximum speed of 630 mph. The RAF exchanged its Lincoln piston bombers for the Valiant, the first of the V-bombers, and this was followed by the cresent-wing Victor and the delta-wing Vulcan.

In Russia the Tu-4 regiments re-equipped with the pure-jet Tu-16, known in the west as Badger, the four prop-jet Tu-20 codenamed Bear, and later the four turbo-jet Bison with a top speed of 620 mph and a range of 7000 miles.

In the United States the delivery of the deterrent had passed to the B-52 Stratofortress, a bomber on the same scale as the B-36, but with eight turbofan engines giving it a top speed of 630 mph and an unrefuelled range of more than 12,000 miles. A section of the Strategic Air Command went supersonic with the Convair Hustler, a medium delta-wing bomber with a speed of 1300 mph and an operational radius of 1200 miles. Plans were in hand for SAC to re-equip with the North American B-70 long range supersonic bomber but although two examples were built the machine did not progress beyond the prototype stage.

France became the fourth nuclear power, followed in due course by China. The French deterrent was mounted on the Dassault Mirage IV, a light supersonic bomber with a range sufficient only for 'one-way' missions into the heart of Russia. In Britain supersonic bomber development terminated abruptly with the cancellation of the TSR-2, and the Royal Air Force maintains its nuclear punch with the obsolescent Vulcan.

**Convair B-58 Hustler**
The world's first supersonic bomber demonstrated its capability over a long distance by hurtling from New York to Paris in just over three hours in 1961.

## Boeing 707
The American jet transport era began when the 707 prototype flew on July 15, 1954. Since then, the 707 family of airliners has changed the whole nature of air travel, bringing reliable, comfortable flying to millions who previously journeyed by land and sea.

## Vickers (BAC) VC10
Britain's largest jet airliner featured tail-mounted engines, leaving the wing surface clear to confer exceptional take-off performance from small airfields.

### Hawker Siddeley Trident

Jets for shorter inter-city routes revert to the three-engined fashion of the early pioneer days. The Trident 3 shown here has a fourth small engine to boost take-off power. In 1965, a British European Airways Trident made the first 'blind landing' automatic touchdown on a commercial service.

## Jet Airliners in World-wide Service

### Boeing 737

The twin-engined member of the Boeing jetliner family gives large airliner comfort over short distances.

# Jetliners

The coming of the jetliner marked the coming of age of air travel. Now that the Atlantic could be crossed in six hours in luxuriously fitted cabins, offering the comfort and cuisine of a five-star hotel—plus a viewing of the latest motion picture—the ocean liner ploughing through surface storms at 25 knots seemed as outdated as a Model T Ford.

Before long, more people were crossing the Atlantic by air than by sea, and the proud ocean liners were being laid up or relegated to holiday cruising. So great was the boom in air travel that it has been calculated that during 'rush hours' there are enough people airborne between Europe and America to populate a medium-sized city.

On both sides of the Atlantic the aircraft industries geared themselves to meet the demands of the airlines. The Boeing 707 was the undisputed leader, rolling down vast production lines in quantities unprecedented even at the height of the war. In its first version, the 707 seated 130 passengers, but this was soon inadequate. Stretched versions appeared and still the call was for more and more seats. The final 707 version can accommodate 189 passengers in high density seating, while the rival DC-8 has been stretched to seat no less than 251. The British aircraft industry, which began the jetliner revolution with the de Havilland Comet, produced the Vickers VC-10 and its development the Super VC-10, with accommodation for up to 175 passengers. Its four Rolls Royce Conway turbofans are mounted in pairs on either side of the rear fuselage, giving the smoothest, quietest ride of any contemporary jetliner.

## Boeing B-47 Stratojet

The Stratojet was a major step forward in bomber design, with the unusual features for its time of engines slung beneath the swept wings in pods and the arrangement of its main landing wheels in tandem under the fuselage (see page 80).

Even when the big jets were firmly established on the long range routes, it was widely believed that the pure jet aeroplane would not be a suitable means of transport over medium or short ranges. It was said, for example, that a machine on the London-Paris run would scarcely have accelerated to maximum speed before it had to slow down in preparation to land. Once again the aviation prophets were mistaken. By the mid-1960s, the prop-jets Viscounts, Vanguards and Electras were giving place to Tridents, Boeing 727s Caravelles and BAC One-Elevens—the new tail-jet generation with two or three turbofans clustered around the rear fuselage.

The Trident brought a new revolution in its wake—automatic landing. Designed to allow jetliners to touch down safely in dense fog without the pilot touching the controls, Autoland has been brought into service in stages over a period of years. Although not yet cleared for completely automatic operation in fog, many thousands of Trident passengers have already been landed by a 'fail-safe' triplicated robot housed in a little black box.

# Modern Supersonic Fighters

That modern fighter aircraft do not conform to any standard pattern will be obvious from a glance at this page. Fighter design has not always been so varied—the single seaters of the Second World War were, with one or two exceptions, remarkable for their similarity to one another. The limiting factor in that period was the heavy piston engine which had to be mounted in the nose of the machine as there was no acceptable alternative to the tractor airscrew. The airscrew diameter of anything up to twelve feet had to be given adequate clearance in the take-off position and this in turn dictated a low wing position in order that the length of retracting under-carriage legs could be kept to a minimum. The pilot was almost invariably positioned a little ahead of the wing trailing edge with a field of view that was limited in flight and almost non-existent on the ground.

The jet turbine changed the picture completely. The low weight of the new power plants meant that they could be mounted almost anywhere on the airframe and early jet fighters

## British Aircraft Corporation Lightning

This Mach 2 interceptor is equipped with infra-red heat-seeking guided missiles and is frequently used in the interception and surveillance of Russian intelligence-gathering aircraft operating around the British coastline.

## Dassault Mirage

One of the most successful military aircraft of all time, the Mirage has been exported from France to many of the world's air forces.

## Sepecat Jaguar

The lightweight Jaguar is built jointly by Britain and France as a tactical support strike aircraft, able to carry a heavy and versatile load of weapons, delivered with great accuracy and guided by sophisticated electronic equipment.

demonstrated their designer's new-found freedom of action. Sometimes jets were mounted under the wings (Me262 and Gloster Meteor) or slung below the nose (Yak 15) or carried in a pod over the rear fuselage (He162). The DH Vampire had the engine behind the pilot, with the jet exhausting behind the trailing edge and the tailplane carried high on twin booms, while the Shooting Star had the engine in the rear fuselage. With the exception of the Yak 15, which was a converted piston engine fighter, and the Me262, which began life with a piston engine mounted in the nose, the pilots of those early jet fighters all sat well forward of the wing and enjoyed superb fields of view both in the air and on the ground.

The first jets had a speed advantage of around 100 mph over their piston-engined contemporaries, but whereas the piston engine had been developed to its limit, the jet was only just beginning. Early engines could deliver about 1500 lb of thrust—fifteen years after the war engines of ten times that power were in production and today fighters such as the Mig23 have twin engines each delivering more than 30,000 lb with afterburning.

The enormously increased power outputs took fighter design first to the speed of sound (around 700 mph at sea level) and then way beyond. The Swedish Draken and the Mirage 5 both have maximum speeds of Mach 2 (1350 mph at 35,000 feet) while the Lightning can reach 1500 mph, or Mach 2·27 at 40,000 feet. But these relatively similar performances are achieved with totally different aerodynamic layouts. The Lightning has sharply swept wing and tail surfaces with twin jet engines mounted one above the other in the rear fuselage. It is a big aeroplane—the loaded weight is around 50,000 lb is not much less than that of a fully loaded Lancaster bomber.

The Mirage 5 is a smaller machine with a loaded weight of about 30,000 lb. It has a *delta* wing, the name deriving from the Greek letter ∧. The wing plan forms an almost perfect triangle and there are no horizontal tail surfaces—the control surfaces on the trailing edge serving both as ailerons and elevators.

The Saab Draken, with a loaded weight of 35,000 lb, is similar in general layout to the Mirage 5 but has a *double-delta*. This is a design compromise which seeks to combine the high speed characteristics of the narrow, highly swept delta with the good low-speed handling characteristics of the moderately swept delta wing. As with the Mirage 5 there is no separate horizontal tail surface and the trailing edge *elevons* serve for both pitch and lateral control.

### Vought-Sikorsky VS-300
Igor Sikorsky designed his first helicopter in Russia in 1909; however it was not until 1940, in the USA, that he constructed and flew a successful machine, the VS-300.

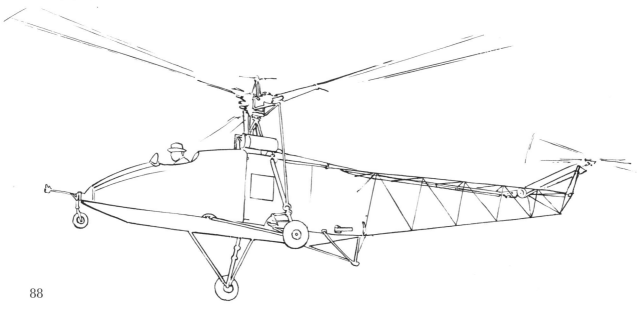

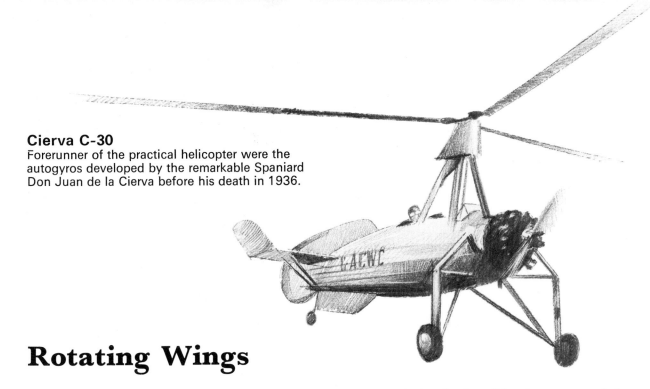

**Cierva C-30**
Forerunner of the practical helicopter were the
autogyros developed by the remarkable Spaniard
Don Juan de la Cierva before his death in 1936.

# Rotating Wings

Although the concept of a rotating wing as a means of developing lift almost certainly originated with the ancient Chinese, it was not until September 1907 that a helicopter, built by Louis and Jacques Breguet, lifted a man into the air for a brief tethered flight. In November of that year Paul Cornu made the first free flight in a tandem rotor machine, but he lacked resources to continue with his experiments. In 1910 Igor Sikorsky constructed two helicopters in Russia, but both were unsuccessful, and for the next thirty years he turned his attention to fixed-wing machines.

In 1927 Juan de la Cierva produced the first really practical rotating-wing aircraft—the Cierva Autogiro. In this machine the nose-mounted engine drove a standard tractor airscrew, while the rotor 'windmilled' in the slipstream. Because there was no connection between the engine and the rotor, the autogiro was not a vertical take-off aircraft, but its take-off run was very much less than that of a conventional fixed-wing machine. The so-called 'jump-start' autogiro had a clutch which allowed the pilot to use engine power to spin the rotor at the moment of take-off—and thus in effect convert it into a helicopter for a brief period.

Autogiros were popular with private pilots in the 1930s and also served in a number of air forces as observation machines. During the war the German navy experimented with man-carrying autogiro kites for observation duties with the U-boat fleet: today the girocopter, direct descendant of Cierva's autogiro, continues to find favour with private pilots, and one girocopter achieved world-wide fame as James Bond's personal transport in the film *You Only Live Twice*.

The first helicopter to achieve sustained flight was the French Breguet-Dorand which flew in 1935. This twin co-axial rotor design set world records in 1936 by climbing to a height of just over 500 feet, remaining airborne for sixty-two minutes and reaching a speed of almost 28 mph. The achievements of the Breguet-Dorand were eclipsed in May 1937 when the Focke-Achgelis Fw61 with twin contra-rotating rotors mounted side-by-side climbed over 11,000 feet and flew for 143 miles. The Fw 61 had a top speed of 76 mph, made the first autorotative (engine off) descent, and made the first indoor helicopter flight. It was not, however, capable of carrying a worthwhile payload, and although a more advanced machine was planned, Focke Wulf had more urgent fixed-wing matters on hand and were forced to abandon helicopter development.

The first really successful helicopter, the VS-300, flew in 1940 with its designer Igor Sikorsky at the controls. After thirty years Sikorsky, now resident in America, had returned

**Sikorsky Sea King**
This anti-submarine and transport helicopter is seen hovering above the Apollo XI command module at the moment of splashdown on its triumphal return from the moon.

### Bell Jet Ranger
A turbine-powered helicopter luxuriously appointed for private use.

### Bell Model 47
Demonstrates how a small helicopter can be employed in the role of aerial crane.

### Bell Iroquois
Dating from 1960, the UH-1 has been used in very large numbers in Vietnam by the US Army. This highly manoeuvrable helicopter has been used for carrying troops into battle, in the armed support rôle and for casualty evacuation.

to helicopter design, a field which his company dominates to the present day. VS-300 was essentially a research tool, but the R-4 which followed it saw service with both the USAF and the RAF in World War Two, and provided an impressive foretaste of the helicopter's unique capabilities.

The helicopter really came into its own in the Korean war, when Sikorsky S-51s and S-55s plucked shot down pilots from behind the enemy lines, carried commando units into action in inaccessible country, and evacuated tens of thousands of wounded men—many of whom would certainly have died without immediate hospital treatment. The 'chopper' had become an essential item of military equipment, but it is doubtful if even its most ardent protagonists at that time could have foreseen how future helicopters would revolutionise tactical warfare. In Vietnam they were to be employed by the thousand, transporting whole divisions into battle, supplying food and amunition, flying in re-inforcements and evacuating wounded men. And from the infantry battle of Vietnam there emerged an entirely new category of military aircraft—the helicopter gunship. It began with Bell Iroquois assault choppers providing covering fire with heavy machine guns. Then rocket and grenade launchers were mounted to suppress enemy strongpoints, and eventually the Hueycobra went into action—a custom-designed gunship with a speed of 220 mph, the agility of a humming bird and fire power equivalent to the broadside of a destroyer.

In civil aviation today, the helicopter is firmly established as airliner, executive transport, airborne ambulance, rescue vehicle and flying crane. It is no longer front page news when a helicopter lifts a new church spire into position, retrieves a crashed aircraft or delivers spare parts and engineers to a crippled ship far out at sea. Police helicopters patrol motorways, chopper mounted television camera give us a birds eye view of sporting events—and the off-shore oil industry on both sides of the Atlantic would almost grind to a halt without the big helicopters that service the oil rigs in every kind of weather.

But of all the multitude of duties carried out as a matter of routine, it is perhaps in the field of emergency services that the helicopter has made its greatest contribution. In earthquake, fire and flood the steady beat of rotors is often the first indication that help is at hand and there is no way of knowing how many thousands of people owe their lives to the speedy arrival of a helicopter.

Since the first flight of the VS-300, helicopter development has been rapid and the rate of progress is, if anything, accelerating. In Russia the giant Mil-12 can carry a payload of forty tons, while in the United States the co-axial rotor Sikorsky S-69, due to fly in 1973, is expected to reach a maximum speed of 345 mph.

**Sikorsky XR-4**
The XR-4 was delivered in May, 1942. Production models of this design became the first helicopters to see service in World War 2.

**Mi-12**
This Russian giant, the world's largest helicopter,
appeared in 1971 and soon proved itself by lifting
a load of more than forty tons to a height of
seven thousand feet.

# Strike Aircraft

Two of todays most successful land-based strike aircraft, the Buccaneer and the Phantom II
both originated in naval specifications. The Buccaneer was ordered by the Royal Navy and
flew for the first time in 1958. In its Mk 2 version it was re-engined with Spey turbofans
and delivered in quantity to Royal Navy squadrons and to the maritime command of the
South African Air Force.

Royal Air Force interest in the Buccaneer came about as a result of the cancellation of
the supersonic TSR2 bomber. The British government of the day had ordered the untried
American F111 to fill the gap left by TSR2, but a series of in-flight failures combined with
performance shortcomings led in turn to the cancellation of F111. Hope was then pinned on
the Anglo-French swing wing bomber, but that too proved a non-starter. Eventually an
Anglo-German strike aircraft, the Panavia 200, was ordered for large scale RAF service,
but in the meantime the RAF was left with ageing Canberras quite unsuited to the needs of
modern aerial warfare.

In this situation, the Buccaneer Mk 2 proved an ideal stop-gap. With its extremely robust
construction it can fly below enemy radar scans at speeds very close to Mach 1, the speed of
sound. It can carry up to eight tons of bombs and rockets and its internal fuel tanks give it a
radius of action of 550 miles—a range that can be greatly extended by in-flight re-fuelling
from a Victor tanker.

The Phantom II also flew for the first time in 1958 and was ordered in quantity as a
shipboard interceptor and strike aircraft. It soon established itself as the most advanced
fighter bomber in existence, with a maximum speed in excess of 1500 mph and an ordnance-
carrying capability of up to eight tons. It was ordered for service with the USAF, the
West German and Israeli air forces. A modified version with Rolls Royce Spey turbofans
was ordered in quantity for service with both the Royal Air Force and the Royal Navy.

By the end of 1970, 4000 Phantoms had been delivered. Today, fourteen years after its
first flight, the Phantom II retains it position as the most potent strike fighter in service.

**Lockheed F-104 Starfighter** (*top*)
Called the 'manned missile', this fighter with
incredibly small, thin wings was ordered by the
USAF, flying for the first time in 1954. The F-104
has served with many air arms, including Japan,
as shown here.

**McDonnell F-4 Phantom** (*centre*)
Portrayed in the colours of the West German Air
Force, the F-4 has been developed, since its design
in 1953, into one of the most versatile and potent
strikers in service today.

**Republic F-105 Thunderchief** (*bottom*)
Entering USAF service in 1959, the 'Thud' served
with distinction in the Vietnam conflict, flying more
than 75% of all the strike missions during the
years 1964-69.

# Cargo by air

**Bristol Freighter**
The first flying car ferry was popular with
post-war motorists travelling from Britain to Europe.

Aeroplanes have been carrying freight of one sort or another for more than fifty years. In the early days, air cargo was not taken too seriously. Urgent mail and other high-priority goods might yield a worthwhile return, but even the most ardent advocate of the commercial aeroplane would have hesitated to forecast that air freight would one day become big business.

The large-scale military airlifts of World War 2, and more particularly the two-and-a-half-million tons of freight air-lifted into Berlin during the great blockade, proved that under the right conditions the carriage of cargo by air could be a commercial proposition.

Aircraft manufacturers began looking at the problem of the specialised aerial freighter. One of the early success stories was that of the Bristol Freighter and the later Super-Freighter. This was a large twin-engined, high-wing monoplane with a fixed undercarriage and a cavernous square-section fuselage entered by clam-shell doors in the nose. The availability of the means of transport generated the trade: a car-ferry service across the English Channel proved a money spinner because it saved the holiday-bound motorist from the time-consuming process of loading his car onto a cross-channel steamer and then unloading it at the other side—to say nothing of the prospect of an uncomfortable two or three-hour crossing of a singularly unpredictable stretch of water. A Super-Freighter could accommodate three large cars together with their occupants and sundry scooters and motor cycles, and deliver them to the other side in around twenty minutes. Like other surface transporters before and since, the operators of the cross-Channel steamers began to feel the cold wind of competition.

If an aeroplane can make a profit, then a bigger aeroplane will make a bigger profit, seems to be law in the commercial aviation. The next step in the car-ferry business was obviously a machine which would carry six cars instead of three and as such a machine was not in immediate prospect from the airframe manufacturers, an enterprising firm in Southend set about converting surplus Douglas DC-4s. The result was the Carvair, an unlikely-looking machine in which the crew sat in a flight deck raised above the redesigned clam-shell nose.

Today, aircraft designers are thinking in terms of transporting cars on a mammoth scale—not this time the vehicles of holidaying motorists, but new cars straight out of the factory. The Lockheed L-500, a civil freighter development of the C-5A Galaxy, has been offered to General Motors as a means of cutting delivery time between Detroit and the American west coast from eight days to under four hours. Even greater savings in delivery times could be made by flying export cars across the Atlantic.

Back in the 'golden days' of flying before World War 1, Moore-Brabazon—later Lord Brabazon of Tara—once took a pig for a flight as a joke after a friend had referred to the proverb 'if pigs could fly'. Later, in 1924, KLM Royal Dutch Airlines used a Fokker F.111 to transport a prize bull from Rotterdam to Paris—this time as a commercial undertaking. That pair of four-legged pioneers was the vanguard of millions of animals of every shape and size which have since joined the ranks of air travellers. Race-horse owners soon discovered that such temperamental creatures were far less disturbed by a short air journey than by a long and often rough sea crossing. Moore-Brabazon would no doubt have been astounded to learn that the day would come when pigs not only flew regularly but were, on occasions joined by an elephant, a giraffe or even a killer whale. So many animals pass through London/Heathrow that the British Airports Authority set up an animal hostel to see to their welfare —their most famous visitors to date having undoubtedly been Chi-Chi and An-An, the giant pandas, in the course of their much-publicised London-Moscow courtship.

Air freight is a rapidly expanding industry. Major international airports have established computerised cargo-handling bases and it is anticipated that in the next decade the commercial return on carriage of cargo will outstrip that on carriage of passengers. Already, in terms of value of goods shipped in and out, London/Heathrow has assumed the position of Britain's number one port.

During the Berlin Airlift, Dakotas were taking off loaded to the gunwales with coal because, in the context of the blockade, the price was right. With the tremendous carrying capacity of the Lockheed L-500—one hundred and sixty tons of payload over 3000 miles at more than 500 mph—the transport of bulk goods such as coal, oil and grain is now being considered as a viable commercial proposition.

Fifteen years ago, the passenger-carrying jetliner relegated the ocean 'Queens' to the second division; we may, in the not-far-distant future, see a similar process affect cargo ships.

### Junkers G38
A Lufthansa G38 loading mail in 1933.

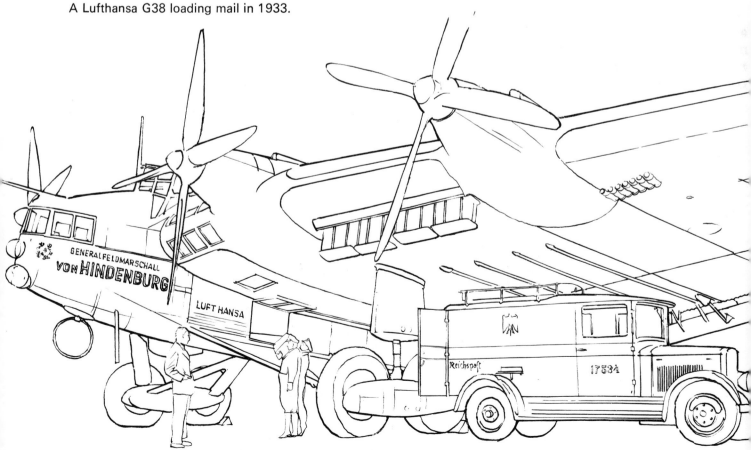

# Submarine Hunters

## Avro Shackleton
Forerunner of the Nimrod, the piston-engined Shackleton roamed the world for more than two decades, watching over Britain's maritime trade routes.

## Hawker Siddeley Nimrod
The twenty-year-old basic airframe of the Comet airliner took on a new lease of life in 1969 when the Nimrod joined the RAF. The world's first jet-powered submarine hunter carries a comprehensive range of detection devices and weapons.

## Lockheed P-3 Orion
Shown here in the colours of the Royal Norwegian Air Force is a submarine hunter powered by Allison turboprops. Like Nimrod, it is derived from a civil airliner design. The Orion is the standard US Navy land-based anti-submarine aircraft. The first protype flew in 1959.

# Light Aircraft

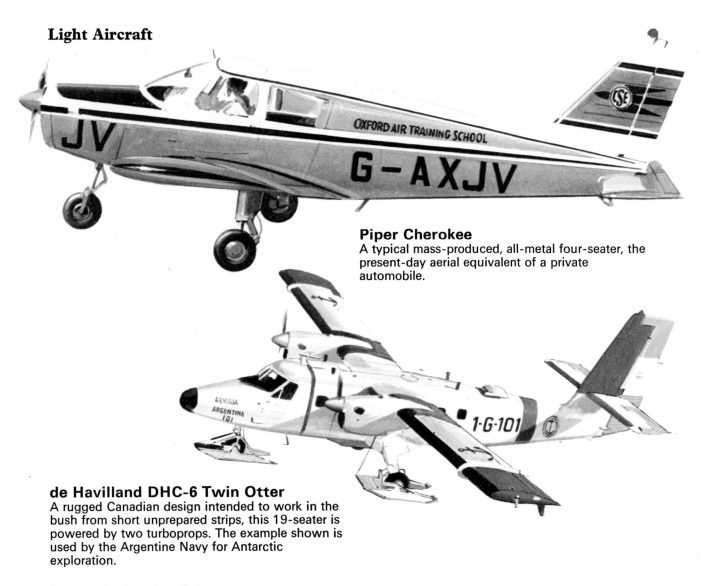

### Piper Cherokee
A typical mass-produced, all-metal four-seater, the present-day aerial equivalent of a private automobile.

### de Havilland DHC-6 Twin Otter
A rugged Canadian design intended to work in the bush from short unprepared strips, this 19-seater is powered by two turboprops. The example shown is used by the Argentine Navy for Antarctic exploration.

### Dassault Fan Jet Falcon
Small high-speed passenger jets have been developed to fill the need for an airliner in miniature to carry executives so that they can be independent of airline routes and schedules. An eight-seat French Fan Jet Falcon is illustrated.

# Aircraft at work

**Antonov An2**
Mainstay of Russian agricultural aviation.

The enormous expansion of the air transport industry in half a century is taken for granted by the general public. Even the sight of a Jumbo Jet hauling four hundred passengers out of an international airport scarcely occasions a second glance.

Much less well-known and understood are the multitude of other duties performed by specialized aircraft every day in the service of industry, agriculture and commerce.

Of particular importance are aerial photography techniques developed for wartime reconnaisance and now employed to build up photo-mosaics of town and country which can be used by cartographers to draw maps which are more accurate than those based on traditional ground survey methods. The very high standard of accuracy achieved in this way is vital in the planning of new community projects such as motorways, new towns, river flood control. Aircraft equipped with highly specialized photographic and electro magnetic apparatus are also being used in the search for mineral deposits and new oil and natural gas fields. Other machines, such as the rugged BN2 Islander, are being used by fishery research organisations to monitor the size and location of fish shoals and collate the results with data on weather, tide and coastal topography: the aim of such research being to increase the yield from the sea while at the same time preventing over-exploitation of resources.

Farmers have been using aircraft for many years to spread pesticides and fertilizer. The pilots of agricultural aircraft are a special breed—the job is often dirty and is always dangerous as it involves very low flying coupled with the need to make tight, steeply banked turns close to the ground and in frightening proximity to trees, power lines and other obstacles. The aircraft, too, are becoming a special breed. Originally, the farm aeroplane was a converted trainer with a chemical hopper in a blanked-off front cockpit, but aircraft manufacturers are finding it worth their while to develop such machines as the Airtruk and Snow Commander which can lift a ton of chemicals. In Africa, pest control aircraft are providing the first real check on the age-old plague of the locust and elsewhere camera-equipped machines using specially developed infra-red colour film are being used in trials to detect crop disease at an early enough stage for it to be eradicated. Another of man's ancient enemies is forest fire. To combat this, light fire patrol aircraft search for any sign of smoke or flame. At the first indication of fire, forest fire fighters are air-lifted to the scene and if necessary the 'water bombers' are scrambled. These are flying boats or amphibians like the Canadair CL 215 which can fill its water tanks by skimming across the surface of a lake near to the seat of the fire and then deluging the blaze with several tons of water dropped from tree-top height.

In business use, the aeroplane has a rather more glamorous image. The executive jet or helicopter with its colourful livery has a firmly established place in large commercial organisations, saving valuable time for highly-paid personnel and transporting essential components

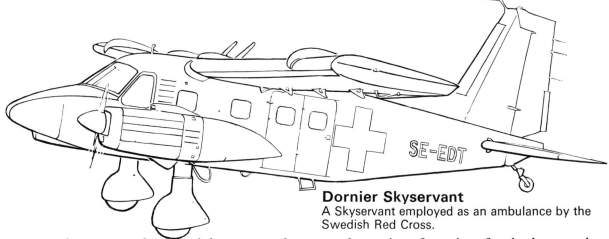

**Dornier Skyservant**
A Skyservant employed as an ambulance by the Swedish Red Cross.

from one plant to another. Aerial transport between the various factories of a single organisation is now of great importance to the aircraft industry itself. Airbus Industrie is an example: the A-300B Airbus is the product of a five-nation consortium of France, Germany, Britain, Holland and Spain. The major fuselage components are built by MBB and VFW-Fokker in Bremen and Hamburg; major wing structures are assembled at Chester by Hawker Siddeley, while the tailplane, flying control surfaces, flaps, slats and doors, etc., are manufactured by Fokker in Amsterdam and Casa in Seville. These components are then transported to the assembly lines at Toulouse. Major items, such as the fuselage and wing sections posed a considerable problem. It was solved by a 'Super-Guppy', a much modified Boeing Stratocruiser with propeller turbines in place of the standard piston engines and with a vast airship-like fuselage. The Super-Gruppy is operated by a French airline and is hired out for the Airbus and Concorde projects. In the United States, similar Super-Gruppys are employed in transporting sections of the Saturn/Apollo launch vehicles from the factory to the launching site at Cape Kennedy.

Other dramatic examples of the working aeroplane are provided by the many flying doctor and ambulance services around the world. The flying doctor idea was pioneered in Australia, where outback farm families were often separated from the nearest town by hundreds of miles. The answer was provided by rugged two or three-motor aircraft able to operate from small dirt airstrips, coupled with the transeiver—a pedal operated transmitter and receiver in every homestead. The success of the first Flying Doctor experiments led to the establishment of a network of services across Australia and the idea quickly spread to other continents. In Africa, the aerial ambulance and airborne doctor services are firmly established with STOL aircraft such as the Islander.

On a less serious note, working aeroplanes also serve the entertainment industry, giving joy rides at air displays and at the seaside, performing spectacular solo and formation aerobatics, and even taking part in aerial advertising—broadcasting over loudspeakers, towing banners, skywriting with smoke trails and dropping leaflets. Aeroplanes, together with helicopters and small non-rigid airships, provide platforms for movie and television cameramen to give viewers a 'bird's eye view' of horse racing, off-shore powerboat contests and similar large-scale sporting events.

**de Havilland Tiger Moth**
Widely used for recreational flying.

## Aermacchi M.B.326

A tandem two-seat basic trainer, the Italian M.B. 326 is in service with a number of air forces, including the Royal Australian Air Force shown here.

## Hawker Siddeley Gnat

The standard two-seat advanced trainer of the RAF, known throughout the world as the mount of the Red Arrows aerobatic team.

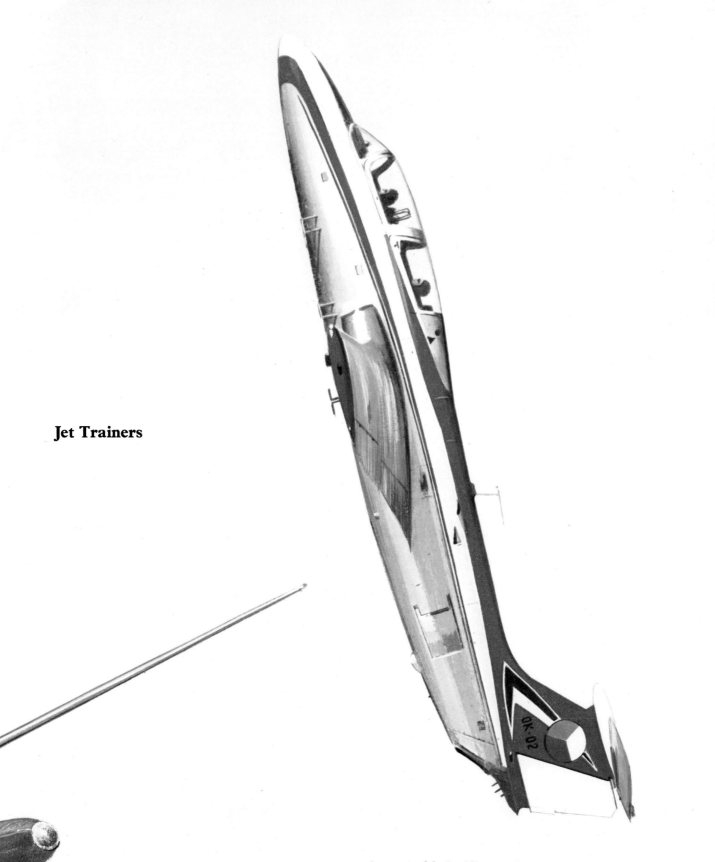

**Jet Trainers**

### Aero L-29 Delfin
The Delfin is the standard jet trainer in the Air
Force of its native Czechoslovakia. After
competition, it was selected for the air forces of the
Soviet Union, Bulgaria, East Germany, Egypt and
Hungary.

# Military Airlifts

The history of military airlifts could be said to go back to Napoleonic days, when there were reports of personnel and supplies being carried into and out of beleaguered cities by hydrogen balloon. The first large-scale airlift was the German invasion of Crete—described on pages 52-53—in which 500 three-motor transports landed an army and supplied it until victory had been achieved.

Later in the war, even more remarkable feats of air-lifting were performed by the Luftwaffe in support of Stalingrad, by the allies in the invasion of Europe, and in Asia by the pilots who flew supplies 'over the hump' into China.

But the most famous air lift of all took place after the end of World War 2. The Berlin Airlift, although flown partly by civilian airliners chartered from America and western Europe, was essentially a military operation carried out for a military purpose—the protection of the West Berlin population from domination by the armies of the Soviet Union.

At midnight on June 18, 1948, Russia suspended road and rail links between West Germany and the western zone of Berlin, and the Berlin Blockade had begun. At first sight, the problems of sustaining the population of a major city by air seemed overwhelming, but by early July the first stop-gap airlift had lifted the immediate threat of starvation from the Berliners. Before the blockade, normal surface freight had totalled some 13,500 tons per day and it was estimated that at least 4500 tons per day would be needed to sustain the city.

At first, the brunt of the flying was carried by USAF and RAF Dakotas, but these elderly twin-engined transports were not suitable for bulk freight. The USAF brought in Skymaster and Constellation four-motor transports and the RAF sent Yorks, the transports version of the Lancaster bomber. But still the need was for more and more transports. Civil aircraft and crews were chartered and at military airfields across West Germany, vast queues of transport aircraft could be seen moving slowly around perimeter tracks awaiting their turn for take off.

The air lift achieved its aim and Berlin was saved, but the lessons of the great blockade were not forgotten. New military transports, like the Douglas C124 Globemaster II and the later C133 Cargomaster were ordered into production while still larger and faster machines began to take shape in the design offices.

The Cargomaster was a giant among aircraft when it first went into service, but today it would look puny alongside a Lockheed Galaxy. Currently the largest aeroplane in the world, the C-5A Galaxy can carry a payload considerably greater than the fully loaded weight of a Cargomaster. It has room for 380 men with all their equipment, or two battle tanks, or ten Pershing missiles complete with towing and launching vehicles. In civil guise, it can accomodate 1000 passengers and with maximum payload it can cruise for 3000 miles at 530 mph.

**Lockheed C-5 Galaxy**
The world's largest aircraft entered USAF service in 1969 to provide a new dimension in heavy logistics capability. The payload of men, supplies, vehicles is 265,000 lb for a range of 2500 miles, in a cargo hold 144 feet long. During the withdrawal from Vietnam, one C-5 carried a single load of twenty-two light helicopters.

**Flight Deck of HMS Ark Royal**
Seen aboard the Royal Navy's last operational carrier are a Buccaneer low-level strike aircraft, three Phantom fighters and three turbo-prop Gannet early warning radar patrol machines. Overhead are two Sikorsky-designed helicopters built in Britain by Westland: the Sea King and the Wessex.

# Spy in the Sky

One of the rôles of the aviator in military service has always been that of aerial observer. As with the most forms of espionage, the operations of the 'spy in the sky' have been little publicised but on many occasions the intelligence gathered in this way has materially affected the outcome of military operations.

The earliest military aeronauts, in Napoleonic times, observed enemy troop dispositions from captive balloons. At the start of World War 1 in 1914, the aeroplane was used exclusively in the scouting rôle, and although aerial combat and ground attack rôles were soon undertaken, the name Fighting Scout was to endure into the 1920s.

Between the wars, both the British and the Germans indulged in clandestine reconnaisance of each other's territories, using private aircraft and airliners as a cover. In May 1939, the Luftwaffe sent the Graf Zeppelin to investigate the British radar chain. In dense cloud the airship navigator lost his bearings. In a radioed message to Berlin he estimated his position as some miles off the Yorkshire coast—and caused considerable amusement in British tracking stations where operators were watching the huge ship hovering over Hull!

During World War 2, photographic reconnaisance and the subsequent interpretation of the results became a highly-developed science. It was able to locate and identify airfields, factories and troop concentrations. Heavy traffic using an insignificant country lane could lead to the discovery of a vital underground installation—and equally the lack of tyre tracks might expose a decoy factory built of wood and canvas.

Perhaps the greatest triumph of photo-reconnaisance in the 1939-1945 war was the discovery of the German secret weapons V-1 and V-2. The subsequent attacks on the research station at Peenemünde delayed the deployment of both weapons by many months and later, when the V-weapons were being installed in France and Belguim, photo-recce located the launching sites. Attacks by fighter bombers, medium bombers and heavy bombers so disrupted the V-weapon programme that less than twenty per cent of the planned launching actually took place, and what could have been a major threat to allied victory became just another trial for the inhabitants of London and its approaches.

After the war, aerial reconnaisance, using new techniques of electronic investigation, assumed an even greater importance. Everyone has heard of the U-2 affair in which a USAF high-altitude photo-recce machine, flown by Gary Powers, was brought down over Russia with a guided missile amid a great deal of publicity. It led to a well-simulated outburst of fury from Mr. Khrushchev and widespread criticism of the United States.

Today, the subsonic U-2 is being superceded by the SR-71, a science-fiction machine that can fly at well over 2000 mph at heights of around 100,000 feet. Less spectacular but of great importance are machines such as the Lockheed EC-121. This is an adaptation of the Super-Constellation airliner with vast electronic housings above and below the fuselage. Cruising at 300 mph, it has a range of 6500 miles and can remain airborne for more than

**Lockheed WV-2 Super Constellation**
The flying radar station.

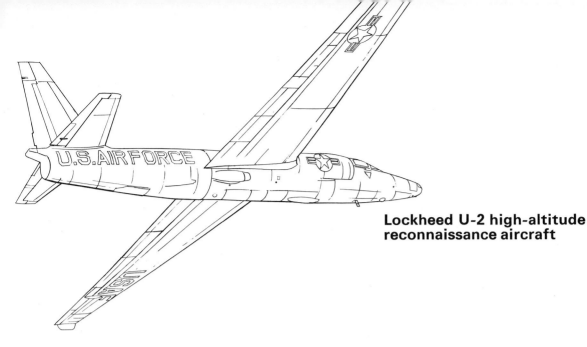

**Lockheed U-2 high-altitude reconnaissance aircraft**

twenty hours. Its operational altitude of 25,000 feet gives it a very wide angle of view and its radar and other observational devices can sweep an area of 40,000 square miles. The crew of 31 collect data on the military capability of actual or potential enemies: they can monitor the air traffic control chatter of a military airbase, or receive and identify radar emissions—distinguishing between defensive radars designed to warn against incoming bombers and missiles, and offensive radars controlling missile complexes. One of the standard electronic reconnaisance operations is known as exercising: this involves feeding a fake signal into an adversary's tracking radar at precise intervals to make him believe that an aircraft or a formation is intruding into his airspace. When defending fighters are launched to intercept the phantom intruder, the crew of the electronic reconnaisance aircraft responsible can watch from a safe distance and gauge the adversary's capability of responding to the threat.

Because the western world is less secretive about such activities, NATO forces in general and the United States in particular are frequently accused of warmongering. It does not seem to be generally recognised that the eastern-block air forces are equally active and that Russian Bear, Badger and Bison reconnaisance bombers make almost daily sorties to the coasts of the United States, Western Europe and Japan. A regular chore for the Lightnings and Phantoms of RAF Fighter Command is to meet an incoming Badger and gently persuade it to turn around and go home. For the most part this is a gentlemanly procedure and the crews wave to each other and even pose for each others cameras. But occasionally the friendly wave is replaced with an air-to-air missile and another spy plane crashes in a blaze of international publicity.

Some years ago, the then President Eisenhower proposed an 'Open Skies' policy which would have allowed reconnaisance aircraft to fly freely anywhere on earth, the aim being to safeguard peace by making it impossible for an aggressor to construct secret installations or concentrate troops. The plan was rejected by the Russians, but in the years since the Eisenhower proposal, space satellites have taken over more and more of the duties of reconnaisance aircraft and today the open skies policy has become a reality, at least as far as unmanned surveillance satellites are concerned. Automatic space-borne cameras already cover virtually every square mile of the earth's surface, recording and reporting the movement of aircraft, ships and tanks. In the near future, manned space vehicles will be stationed in permanent earth orbit—spies in space with high powered telephoto cameras, heat sensitive devices and high definition radars capable of recording military data by night or by day, in clear skies or through the densest cloud.

**Avro Vulcan**
The delta-shaped wing distinguished the unarmed
Vulcan bomber which equipped the RAF's V-force
from 1956 until the responsibility for the delivery of
strategic nuclear weapons passed to the Polaris
submarines of the Royal Navy in 1969.

# The RAF
# at work today

## Handley Page Victor
Another RAF V-bomber which has been adapted for strategic reconnaissance duties and in-flight refuelling. A Victor is seen here about to pass fuel to a **Hawker Siddeley Buccaneer** which has replaced the veteran Canberra in strike squadrons of the RAF.

## Lockheed C-130 Hercules
The Hercules has been flying since 1954, serving with many air forces and some civil operators. Powered by four turboprops, it has proved an extremely versatile tactical transport capable of carrying bulky loads to rough airstrips on the battlefield.

# Korea, Vietnam and the Six-day War

The war in the air in Vietnam and the aerial fighting during the 'Six-Day War' between Israel and the Arab states, provide a striking contrast between partial failure and total success in the application of air power.

At first sight, the Vietnam war would have seemed to have posed the Americans and their South Vietnamese allies with no more of a problem than had been faced and overcome by the United Nations forces in South Korea. But in fact, the situation was totally different. In the barren hills of Korea, there had been no place to hide from the ubiquitous jet fighter patrols. In daylight, nothing could move without risking immediate attack, and even at night B-26 bombers on free intruder patrols harrassed Chinese and North Korean convoys on the exposed mountain roads.

In Vietnam, on the other hand, a sea of green foiliage covers the jungle trails and hides the tens of thousands of peasants with bicycles and mules who carry the arms and ammunition to sustain North Vietnamese divisions fighting south of the 'Demilitarised' Zone. A bicycle with a recoiless rifle tied to the handlebars is not a suitable target for a Phantom, and the area bombing of a trail network by B-52 formations causes little more than temporary inconvenience. The holes are soon filled in and then the human chain is on the move once again.

Even the bombing of targets in North Vietnam appears to have had little effect. Ample labour is available for the speedy repair of roads, bridges and rail tracks, and in a matter of hours after a raid the supplies are rolling south once again. The source of those supplies, the factories which manufacture the rockets, guns and ammunition, are safe from American bombs, behind the borders of China and the Soviet Union.

In the forward battle areas, air power *has* been used with dramatic effect, and entirely new fighting tactics have been evolved. One example of this is the use of massed formations of assault helicopters to carry men to battle, to sustain them in action and to fly out casualties almost as soon as they are wounded. Another Vietnam development is the attack helicopter or gunship, a fast, highly-manœuvrable machine capable of delivering a massive weight of fire onto a pinpoint target. Both the assault helicopter and the gunship are factors likely to affect military thinking far beyond the boundaries of Vietnam.

Fixed-wing air support for allied troops in Vietnam has been provided by a wide variety of aircraft types ranging from the 1945-vintage Skyraider to the latest mark of Phantom. One type which received its baptism of fire over Vietnam is the North American Rockwell OV-10A Bronco. The Bronco, a COIN or counter-insurgency machine, went into action for the first time in 1968. It is a simple, rugged aircraft requiring a minimum of maintenance and able to absorb a great deal of battle damage and still keep fighting and flying.

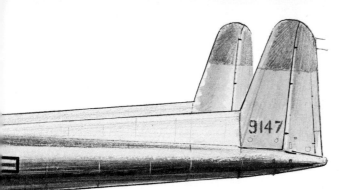

### Fairchild C-119 Boxcar
An armada of C-119 Boxcars of the USAF from Japan supported United Nations ground forces during the conflict in Korea (described on pages 72-73), parachuting men and supplies round the clock throughout the campaign.

The Six Day War fought by Israel in June 1967 was a classic example of the pre-emptive strike. For some days prior to June 5, 1967, President Nasser had directed a war of nerves against Israel, culminating in large-scale troop movements and a notice to quit to the United Nations observers who were supposed to be keeping the peace. No one could doubt Nasser's intention and it seemed that there was nothing to do but wait for the blow to be struck.

Instead Israel struck first. Mirage fighters and Vautour bombers came in from the sea just after the Egyptian dawn patrol had landed and when the bulk of the Egyptian air force was sitting down to breakfast. At air bases across the length and breadth of the country the story was the same. Specially designed 'concrete dibber' rocket bombs pitted the runways, and cannon and rocket fire ripped into neat rows of Russian built fighters and bombers. Within an hour the powerful Egyptian air force had virtually ceased to exist—by midnight on June 6, Egypt had lost 319 operational warplanes and helicopters, all but a handful of which had been destroyed on the ground in the initial strikes.

Deprived of air cover and subject to incessant attack by unopposed Israeli fighter bombers, the Egyptian armies in Gaza and Sinai were routed by the Israeli armour.

The victory was owed almost entirely to the brilliant use of air power, coupled with superb airmanship by Israeli pilots and unprecedented feats of servicing performed by ground crews who refuelled and re-armed aircraft in a matter of minutes.

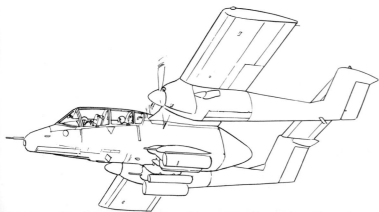

### North American Rockwell Bronco
The Bronco was developed specifically to live and work on the battlefield in close support for ground troops. It is used in the forward air controller rôle, for ground attack, helicopter escort, casualty evacuation and armed reconnaissance.

113

## Boeing 747 (*above*)

The giant Boeing 747 entered service in January, 1970. Taking off at a weight of 710,000 lb (385 tons), the 747 has accommodation for up to 490 passengers cruising at 625 mph. Seven tanks in the wings carry up to 51,000 gallons of fuel for the four turbofan engines. While taxiing, the two pilots and engineer sit 29 feet above ground level. A cabin crew of ten or more is carried to attend to the needs of the passengers. An upstairs lounge area is provided at the rear of the hump on the forward fuselage.

Whisperliner

**The Jumbos**

### Lockheed Tri-Star (*below*)

Designed to cope with the anticipated traffic demands of the 1970s and beyond, the wide-bodied Tri-Star can carry up to 400 passengers over distances of more than 3500 miles. This American airframe is powered by three British Rolls Royce RB211 high bypass-ratio turbofans rated at 42,000 lb of maximum take-off thrust. The advanced technology of this engine has ensured a low noise level up to 75% less annoying to the human ear than the first generation of jet transports.

# The Jumbos

When the Boeing 707 first came into service in 1958 it was regarded by many air transport experts as a white elephant—it was too big and no airline would be able to fill the 130 seats. By the mid 1960s, however, the passenger capacity of the latest 707 had risen to 189, and a stretched version of the DC-8 could accomodate 251—and it was clear that these machines were already too small for the rapidly expanding air transport industry. And so the Jumbo was born.

Although the name Jumbo-jet has become inseparably associated with the Boeing 747, the concept of the wide-body jetliner applies to a whole new family of aircraft. First of these was the Lockheed Galaxy, a military transport potentially capable of lifting 1000 passengers across the Atlantic. As a pioneer the Galaxy suffered protracted development problems with both engines and airframe. In solving these problems, at a cost of hundreds of millions of dollars over and above the original estimates, Lockheed paved the way for other manufacturers to reap the rewards. The Boeing 747 is now in world-wide service as a passenger transport accommodating up to 490 passengers in nine-abreast seating, and its all-cargo version seems set to revolutionise the air-freight market.

Although marginally smaller than the Galaxy, the 747 is still a giant by any standards. Its wings have greater sweepback than the Boeing 707 giving it an economical cruising speed some 40 mph greater than it smaller stablemate. These very high subsonic cruising speeds in turn demand enormous power and the four 'new generation' turbo-fans each deliver 43,500 lb of thrust, compared with the 18,000 lb delivered by the most powerful 707 engines.

But increased power is only one aspect of the revolution in technology represented by the new turbo-fan engines. Large diameter enclosed fans are used to propel masses of cold air from the jet exhausts, augmenting the thrust and muffling the hot supersonic exhaust gases. This, combined with other methods of sound insulation, means that a Boeing 747 creates less noise than a 707 despite the fact that it carries almost three times as many passengers. Reduced noise levels, less exhaust smoke because of more efficient combustion, and fewer aeroplanes carrying an equivalent passenger load are all very important factors at a time when the public are becoming ever more aware of the nuisance caused by noise and smoke.

Following close on the heels of the Boeing 747 has come the McDonnell Douglas DC-10 and the Lockheed Tri-Star, big tri-motor airliners with a 40,000 lb thrust turbofan under each wing and a third in the tail. Seating up to 343 passengers in nine-abreast cabins, the new tri-jets offer a high standard of passenger comfort coupled with unrivalled economy of operation.

A-300 B Airbus

# Close Support on the Battlefield

In World War 1, pilots soon learned to create alarm and despondency among opposing troops by straffing with machine guns and anti-personnel bombs. The hammering machine guns and explosions were bad enough, but it was soon realised that a large part of the effectiveness of such attacks lay in the demoralising howl of aircraft engines at full throttle.

The Germans remembered the value of noise when they set about the creation of the Luftwaffe in the 1930s. The Stuka, a noisy aeroplane in its own right, was fitted with sirens to add to the ear splitting effect of its approach and the scream of the Stuka was heard with dread from one side of Europe to the other.

World War 2 taught that ordinary interceptors armed with bombs and rockets could create havoc in attacks on pin-point targets only yards ahead of friendly troops—and could look after themselves if enemy fighters appeared. Allied forces pushing east after D-Day developed a technique whereby a ground controller in the front line could call down a strike from a 'Taxi rank' circling above and talk the pilot onto the target. Particularly potent in this guise was the Hawker Typhoon which came to be known to the troops as the Tiffybomber.

When the jet fighter began to replace the wartime propeller-driven machines it was natural that designers should give as much thought to ground attack as to aerial combat. We have seen how Shooting Stars and Thunderjets routed the Communist ground forces in Korea—and they, it must be remembered were first-generation jets with limited engine power. The latest strike fighters, such as the Jaguar now going into service with the RAF and the French air force, can carry several tons of bombs and rockets which they can deliver with pin-point accuracy.

Although the Jaguar has excellent take-off and landing characteristics, it must operate from bases that are some distance from the front line and there is therefore an unavoidable delay between a request for air support and the delivery of bombs on the target. For this reason, military aviation experts all over the world are watching the Royal Air Force and the United States Marine Corps with keen interest. These two services are pioneering the most potent close-support weapons system ever devised—the Hawker Siddeley Harrier. The Harrier is a single-seat strike fighter with a maximum speed of just under Mach 1 and a tactical radius of 400 miles, carrying up to 5000 lb of offensive stores. In all this, the Harrier is an orthodox fighter bomber: where it differs from every other fighter in service anywhere in the world is in its VTOL capability—Vertical Take-off and Landing. The Harrier's single jet engine exhausts through four swivelling nozzles. By moving a handle in the cockpit the pilot can direct thrust either downwards, backwards or forwards, allowing the machine to rise vertically into the air, hover, fly backwards at 40 mph or forwards at 730 mph. It can hide in a forest clearing for re-arming and re-fuelling and then streak into battle at the speed of sound.

## Hawker Siddeley Harrier

The world's first vertical take-off strike fighter has brought a new dimension in close support to the armies in the field. The Harrier is able, as shown here, to drop into an isolated forest clearing or any such confined space, giving incredible mobility as it is free of prepared concrete runways. Fuel and ammunition are supplied to such forward airstrips by helicopter.

## General Dynamics F-111E

An F-111 of the USAF sweeps low to avoid detection by radar. This potent strike aircraft was the first 'swing wing' to enter service, and after overcoming an unhappy teething period is now deployed in large numbers as part of Nato's air power in Europe.

# Technology for the 1970s

Seventy years after Kitty Hawk, aviation is preparing for the next great stride into the future. The Anglo-French Concorde airliner, now ready to enter service, will halve the flight time across the Atlantic, just as the Comet and 707 halved it fourteen years ago. Another long-discussed development is about to come upon the civil aviation scene—the QSTOL, the letters standing for Quiet Short Take-off and Landing. The design departments of the world's aircraft industries are working flat out to produce an aeroplane which will take off from short airstrips close to city centres creating a minimum of noise and smoke and then carry a hundred or more passengers at 500 mph to another city airport. Typical of the designs currently under discussion is the British Aircraft Corporation project for a four turbofan airliner carrying up to 140 passengers. Because of the high cost of development, the QSTOL liners are almost certain to be international ventures—BAC is discussing its project with Messerschmitt-Bolkow-Blohm of Germany and SAAB of Sweden.

In military aviation, too, new fighters and bombers are being prepared for service. In Europe, the companies which in the last war produced the Spitfire and the Messerschmitt Me109 have joined with an Italian company to form a consortium named Panavia to build the Multi-rôle Combat Aircraft. MRCA, a variable-geometry or swing-wing strike fighter, has been ordered in large numbers for the RAF, West German and Italian air forces.

Further in the future is the North American Rockwell B-1, a supersonic long-range strategic bomber planned to replace the 400 ageing Boeing B-52s in service with the Strategic Air Command. B-1 is a large variable-geometry aircraft designed for low-level operation at the speed of sound or very high altitude attack at more than 1500 mph. Equipped with stand-off missiles which can be launched outside the enemy's perimeter, and with the most sophisticated electronic defence devices, B-1 will supplement long range ballistic missiles for the delivery of the nuclear deterrent, and yet be far more flexible in use than a rocket. The limitation of rockets is that once launched they cannot be recalled. B-1, with its ability to cruise for long periods at low speed and then attack at twice the speed of sound, will pose an almost insuperable problem for a potential enemy.

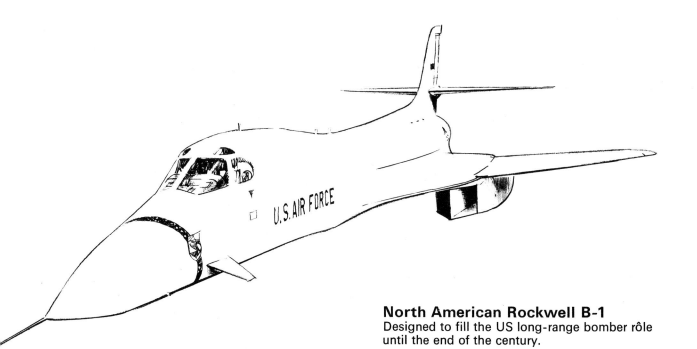

**North American Rockwell B-1**
Designed to fill the US long-range bomber rôle
until the end of the century.

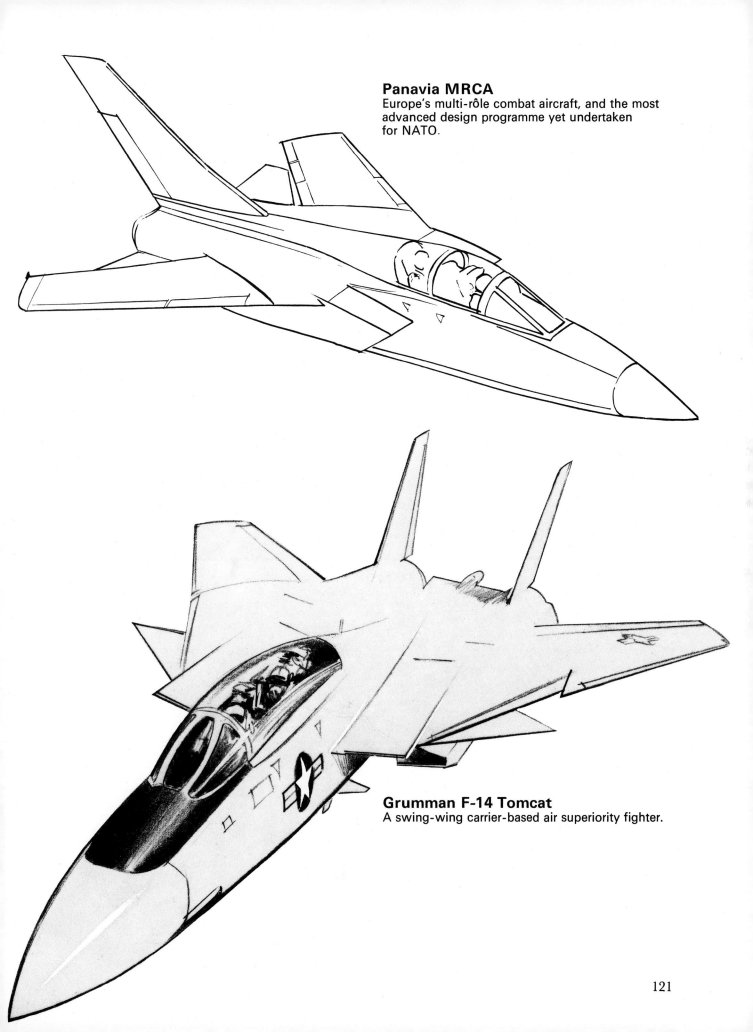

**Panavia MRCA**
Europe's multi-rôle combat aircraft, and the most advanced design programme yet undertaken for NATO.

**Grumman F-14 Tomcat**
A swing-wing carrier-based air superiority fighter.

121

## Aérospatiale-BAC Concorde

Agreements were made between British and French industry in 1962 to construct a supersonic airliner under a joint programme. The Concorde flew in March, 1969, and is depicted here on a visit to Rio de Janeiro in 1971.

# Journey into Space

Rockets, invented by the ancient Chinese, have been used as weapons of war for a thousand years. They were employed in turn by Mongols and Arabs; by French soldiers during the siege of Orleans, and by Indians against the British in the late eighteenth century.

In 1806 British warships bombarded Boulogne with 32-pounder Congreve rockets, and in 1807 Copenhagen was fired by a barrage of 25,000 incendiary rockets. Another barrage in 1812 inspired the reference to 'the rocket's red glare' in the national anthem of the USA.

The nineteenth century saw many improvements in rocket design, including tail fins and 'spin stabilization' induced by aerofoils or angled nozzles, but the rocket's main limitation lay in the black powder that provided its power. In 1903 the Russian physicist Tsiolkovsky designed a rocket which derived its thrust from the mixing and burning of liquid oxygen and liquid hydrogen and his studies included a multi-stage vehicle as big as Saturn V for flight beyond the earth's atmosphere. Tsiolkovsky's rocket designs were never tested, but after the first world war Hermann Oberth in Germany and Robert Goddard in the USA began to put his ideas into practice. By 1935 a 15-foot Goddard rocket weighing 84 lb had climbed one and a half miles and reached a speed of 700 mph.

In Germany, a young student named Wernher von Braun, inspired by the writings of Oberth, began a series of experiments which culminated in the A-4 rocket. In October 1942 an A-4 reached a height of 50 miles and covered a distance of 120 miles. The world was unaware that the space age had dawned, and when the A-4 went into action under its military designation V-2, the people of London could scarcely have been expected to applaud von Braun's achievement.

But achievement it undoubtedly was, and the A-4 was to sire a whole new generation of rocket vehicles that were to revolutionise warfare in the second half of the twentieth century and provide the means for man to explore interplanetary space.

But not all the descendants of von Braun's A-4 have been warlike. In May 1949 an American Viking rocket reached a height of fifty miles—a later Viking rose 158 miles with a payload of 852 lb, and another sent back the first photographs to show clearly the curvature of the earth.

Viking's successor, Vanguard, was designed to launch a 21-lb satellite into orbit, but on October 4, 1957 the Russians launched Sputnik I, a 23-inch sphere weighing 184 lb. American engineers, after a series of failures with Vanguard succeeded in launching a tiny 3¼-lb satellite on March 17, 1958. Thereafter progress was rapid. The Russians, using a huge military booster originally designed to deliver heavy nuclear warheads, carried out a series of 'space spectaculars'. Sputnik II carried the first living creature—the dog 'Laika'— into orbit, while Sputnik III was an automatic space laboratory weighing 2926 lb.

The Americans, hampered by the lack of a large booster, could not match Russia's satellites, weight for weight, but by miniaturising the electronic equipment packed into the Explorer satellites they were able to gather a vast amount of data about the earth's environment. In particular the Explorers charted the radiation belts that surround the earth and extend 45,000 miles into space. These dense concentrations of charged particles are now known as Van Allen belts after the scientist in charge of radiation investigations.

The decade and a half after the launch of Sputnik I saw satellites performing a wide range of duties—providing meteorological data, surveying mineral resources, observing and reporting on astronomical phenomena and, inevitably, observing and reporting military installations. But perhaps the most impressive achievement of satellite technology from the public point of view was in the field of communications. When the Americans launched Telstar, people marvelled at live transatlantic television transmissions—and a musical composition called Telstar found its way into the Hit Parade. Today, with complex communications satellites in synchronous obit 22,300 miles above the surface, viewers take for granted live television transmissions in full colour from any place on earth.

On April 12, 1961 the Russians eclipsed all previous space achievements when Major Yuri Gagarin orbited the earth in a Vostok spacecraft. Once again the Americans had been beaten to the post, but on May 5, 1961, Commander Alan Shepard became the first American in space in the course of a sub-orbital flight in a Mercury spacecraft named Freedom 7. Captain Virgil Grissom followed with a second sub-orbital flight, and on February 20, 1962, Lt Col Glenn flew a Mercury spacecraft named Friendship 7 on a three orbit flight. Friendship 7 was launched by an Atlas booster in full view of world-wide television cameras.

The pace was hotting up and the Russians had not been inactive. On August 6, 1961, Cosmonaut Herman Titov had made a day long orbital flight in Vostok II and on August 11—12, Vostok III and IV were launched and pilots Nikolayev and Popovitch had flown their craft to within three miles of each other. The double launch and near rendezvous was repeated in June 1962 with Vostok V and VI. Vostok V was flown by Lt Col Bykovsky, but the news that electrified the world was that Vostok VI was piloted by Valentina Tereshkova—first woman in space.

The technology of manned space flight progressed rapidly. On October 12, 1964, Voskhod I carried a three-man crew into orbit, and on March 18, 1965, Lt Col Leonov left Voskhod II to make the first 'walk in space'.

The United States launched the first manned Gemini spacecraft on March 23, 1965, with a two-man crew and once again the lift-off took place in a blaze of publicity. Gemini IV followed into orbit on June 3, and James White became the first American to walk in space.

In August 1965 Gemini V remained in orbit for eight days in the course of which the craft was manoeuvred around its second stage booster, proving the ability of spacecraft to change course and formate in flight. The stage had now been set for the first space rendezvous, and on December 15, 1965, the crew of Gemini VII, who had already been in orbit eleven days, were joined by Gemini VI. The two craft approached to within twelve inches of each other before Gemini VI broke formation and re-entered. Gemini VII continued in orbit until December 18, completing 205 orbits and a total of fourteen days in space.

May 25, 1961, must qualify as one of the most significant dates in the history of space travel. On that day the late President John F. Kennedy said: 'I believe that this nation should commit itself to achieving before this decade is out, of landing a man on the moon and returning him to earth.' It was a brave declaration coming as it did the month after Yuri Gagarin's orbit of the earth—at a time when the Soviet Union was demonstrating her clear lead in terms of large boosters and when the United States had yet to complete a manned orbital flight. But from that moment onwards American industry geared itself to achieving a target believed by most people to lie within the realms of science fiction. The Gemini programme, using the military Titan rocket as a booster, proved and practised the techniques that would become routine for the Apollo astronauts: and a team led by Wernher von Braun created the giant Saturn boosters which would thrust man out of this world and into his greatest adventure.

Before man could land on the moon it was essential to learn much more about the nature of the lunar surface. Hampered by earth's dense atmosphere, even the largest telescopes were unable to see objects less than 300 feet across, and many astronomers believed that the surface was covered in a layer of fine dust up to thirty feet in depth, a most serious hazard for a visiting spacecraft.

As early as September, 1959, Russia had crashed a small space probe, Luna II, on to the surface and on October 4. of that year Luna III had sent back television pictures of the moon from a height of 40,000 miles. Luna III's pictures showed little surface detail but they proved that automatic probes could return pictures and data across a quarter of a

'That's one small step for a man, one giant leap for mankind'.
Neil Armstrong
9.56 pm Houston time
July 20, 1969.

million miles of space. America now embarked on the Ranger programme and after a series of failures, Ranger 7 sent back more than 4000 pictures, some showing craters only a few feet across, before plunging to destruction on the surface. Ranger 8 repeated the success and Ranger 9 transmitted live television pictures as it fell on to the moon. Ranger was succeeded by the Lunar Orbiter programme. These craft were put into low orbit, and in 1966 and 1967 sent back detailed pictures of craters, mountains and laval plains.

The next step was to 'soft land' a robot craft on to the surface, and on February 3, 1966, Russia succeeded in bringing Luna IX to a safe landing. Surveyor I soft landed on June 2, 1966, and was followed by Surveyors III, IV and VII. The vast amount of information returned to earth by these craft disproved the dust layer theory and dispelled any doubt about man's ability to land on and return safely from our nearest neighbour in space.

While robot exploration progressed, work was well in hand on the creation of the Apollo moon ship and its Saturn booster. Apollo is a three part vehicle consisting of lunar module, command module and service module. The lunar (excursion) module or LEM weighs fourteen tons and is designed to carry two of the three Apollo astronauts down to a moon landing. It is itself a two part machine with a descent stage and an ascent stage, each with its own liquid fuel motor. The command module is a conical vehicle weighing five tons and seating the three man crew. It remains linked to the twenty-four-ton service module throughout the journey, separating only for the final descent through the earth's atmosphere.

At the start of a mission, Apollo sits on top of a Saturn V booster with the lunar module packed in the top of the third stage. The complete craft stands 353 feet high and weighs 2725 tons—as much as a World War Two destroyer. Saturn's five first stage engines produce seven and a half million tons of thrust and boost the craft to a speed of 6000 mph in 2·5 minutes—consuming fifteen tons of kerosene and liquid oxygen every second.

When the first stage shuts down and falls away, the second stage fires and accelerates the craft to more than 15,000 mph, at which point the third stage ignites for a short burn to place Apollo, with third stage still attached, in parking orbit while all systems are checked and rechecked. When astronauts and ground controllers are completely satisfied the third stage is fired again to boost the ship to some 25,000 mph and is then separated from the service module. At this point the astronauts rotate the command and service modules and retrieve the lunar module from its hangar at the top of stage three. After the LEM has been linked with the command ship, the third stage is allowed to drift away into space and Apollo free-falls towards the moon.

Earth's gravity slows them gradually until they reach the neutral point between the two bodies, after which they accelerate towards the moon. A brief burn of the SM motor injects Apollo into lunar orbit and after more checks two astronauts transfer to the LEM. Still more checks follow and then the LEM separates and begins its descent to the surface some twelve miles below. The astronauts have studied models and photographs of the landing site until they quite literally know it better than their own back yards—which is just as well because the LEM can hover for a mere two minutes above the surface after which it must either land or abort.

On April 21, 1972, the moonship Orion touched down on the Descartes Highlands, and man's fifth exploration of the moon began less than sixty-nine years after Orville's historic touchdown at Kitty Hawk. In less than one life span man has travelled from the sand dunes of Carolina to the rocky mountains of the moon. And the story is only beginning— as another Lunar Rover leaves its tyre tracks in the moondust, other spacecraft are mapping the surface of Mars and yet another is *en route* for a brief appointment with Jupiter, after which it will leave the solar system for ever and fly on into the depths of galactic space.